HOW TO COPE
WITH MENTAL ILLNESS
IN YOUR FAMILY

HOW TO COPE
WITH MENTAL ILLNESS
IN YOUR FAMILY

A Self-Care Guide for
Siblings, Offspring,
and Parents

Diane T. Marsh, Ph.D.
and
Rex M. Dickens

Jeremy P. Tarcher/Putnam
a member of
Penguin Putnam Inc.
New York

Most Tarcher/Putnam books are available at special quantity discounts for bulk
purchases for sales promotions, premiums, fund-raising, and educational needs.
Special books or book excerpts also can be created to fit specific needs.
For details, write or telephone Putnam Special Markets, 200 Madison Avenue,
New York, NY 10016; (212) 951-8891.

Jeremy P. Tarcher/Putnam
a member of
Penguin Putnam Inc.
200 Madison Avenue
New York, NY 10016
www.penguinputnam.com

First Trade Paperback Edition 1998
Published simultaneously in Canada

Library of Congress Cataloging-in-Publication Data

Marsh, Diane T.
    [Troubled journey]
    How to cope with mental illness in your family : a self-care guide
for siblings, offspring, and parents / by Diane T. Marsh and
Rex M. Dickens.—1st pbk. ed.
        p.   cm.
    Originally published: Troubled journey. New York : Jeremy P.
Tarcher/Putnam, 1997.
    Includes bibliographical references and index.
    ISBN 0-87477-923-5 (pbk.)
    1. Mentally ill—Family relationships. 2. Adult children of
dysfunctional families. 3. Self-care, Health. I. Dickens, Rex M.
II. Title.
RC455.4.F3M366   1998   98-12327
362.2'042—dc21   CIP

Book design by Lee Fukui

Printed in the United States of America
10 9 8 7 6 5 4 3 2 1

This book is printed on acid-free paper. ∞

To my sister,
Meredith Kuhn,
and my brothers,
Jerry and Fred Thimme

D. T. M.

To the memory of my brother,
David Dickens

R. M. D.

CONTENTS

FOREWORD

~

I T IS AN HONOR to be asked to write a foreword for Diane Marsh and
Rex Dickens's fine book. Both authors have made major contributions
to the understanding of family members of severe mental illnesses
through their writings, support groups, and active participation in the National Alliance for the Mentally Ill (NAMI). The authors know whereof
they write, and the book reflects the depth and breadth of their experience.

Severe mental illnesses, like large stones thrown in the water, spread
outward in all directions to wash over everyone nearby. The closer the
persons, the larger the waves they experience. The effects of this, as de-
tailed by the authors, are highly variable and run the spectrum from increasing a person's strengths and coping skills to devastation and divorce.
Self-help books such as this necessarily focus more attention on the negative effects, but the authors also cite examples of individuals who have accepted their relative's severe mental illness and moved on with their lives.
One of my favorites is the following young woman whom they describe:

> It had never occurred to me that I should be adversely af-
> fected. I remember standing up in second grade and sharing
> the mental condition of my brother as my contribution to
> Show and Tell. I thought it was the most unique thing about
> my life and certainly better than any hamster!

On the other end of the spectrum are individuals who never recover
from their relative's severe mental illness and for whom it has been called

"a funeral that never ends." Some of these individuals may use it as an excuse for their own shortcomings and wallow in endless years of psychotherapy. One suspects that in some of these cases the person might have been disabled independently of their relative's mental illness.

Having grown into adulthood with a younger sister with schizophrenia, I have long been interested in observing the effects of my sister's illness on my family and myself. My mother died still feeling guilty and wondering if she had somehow caused the disease, an idea firmly implanted in her by sadly misguided psychiatrists in the 1950s and 1960s. My older sister died still embarrassed by her sister's illness, an illness that was not given a name in the polite social circles in which she traveled. My reaction has been to make a career of research on schizophrenia and bipolar disorder, and in fact, approximately half of my senior research colleagues migrated into research because of severe mental illness in a family member.

Dr. Marsh and Mr. Dickens make allowances for such diversity of effects while they provide a practical, well-organized handbook for relatives of severely mentally ill individuals. They take the reader step-by-step through the minefield of possible effects and show the path to safe ground beyond. Support groups for relatives and courses like the "Journey of Hope" are strongly and, I think, appropriately emphasized. The authors even include a section on how to organize such support groups. Individual counseling and psychotherapy are necessary for some relatives but not for many others. But such diversity of response and need should not surprise us. Severe mental illnesses are equal opportunity illnesses, affecting individuals of all strengths, weaknesses, and personality types, and there is no reason why the same thing should not also be true for relatives.

At the end of the book, the authors wisely add a discussion of the mental illness treatment system. In most states, this treatment system is, in reality, a nontreatment system, currently bad and getting worse. The paucity of quality services for severely mentally ill individuals, the frequency of homelessness and violent episodes, the inappropriate jailing of affected individuals—all of these magnify the burden on relatives manyfold. In those few counties and states that have good mental illness treatment services, the effects of these illnesses on relatives is merely a disaster. In the remainder of the counties and states, where services are moderately to grossly inadequate, the effects on relatives become multiple disasters, forever being piled one on top of the other.

It does not have to be this way. Given the fact that more than five million Americans are affected with severe mental illnesses, if and when their millions of relatives and friends organize themselves and demand adequate services, the magnitude of these disasters will be ameliorated considerably. In the meantime, we should continue to use helpful books like *How to Cope with Mental Illness in Your Family* to help us all survive.

E. FULLER TORREY, M.D.,
author of *Surviving Schizophrenia* and *Out of the Shadows: Confronting America's Mental Illness Crisis*

ACKNOWLEDGMENTS

᪣

W‌E COULD NOT have written this book without the involvement of the former Siblings and Adult Children (SAC) Network of the National Alliance for the Mentally Ill (NAMI). NAMI is the largest national mental health advocacy organization, with a central office in Virginia and more than 1,000 state and local affiliates throughout the country. In particular, we are grateful to the SAC group in Pittsburgh, which supported our work in many ways. There are many adult siblings and offspring throughout the country to whom we are thankful: Lisa Ewald Albury, Diane Ammons, Nancy Bracey, Joyce Burland, Jane Cartmell, Martha Churchill, Judy Flanigan, Charles Goldman, Mary Gullekson, Julie Johnson, Karen Kinsella, Nancy Lanoue, Linda Lattner, Ann List, Sharon Murphy, Beth Oakes, Mary Parenti, Annie Saylor, Mary Siebel, LeRoy Spaniol, Jill Taylor, Laura Van Dilla, Marylee Westbrook, and Norm Zuefle. In addition, we express our appreciation to the many family members who contributed to this work anonymously in responding to one of our national surveys.

We would also like to thank other members of NAMI who have supported this book, including Patricia Backlar, Vicky Conn, Robert Coursey, June Husted, Harriet Lefley, Mary Moller, Penny Frese, Vivian Spiese, Mona Wasow, and Rebecca Woolis. Special thanks go to E. Fuller Torrey for agreeing to write the foreword. His family manual, *Surviving Schizophrenia,* has become the essential resource for families who have a close relative with schizophrenia. As a psychiatrist and active member of NAMI, he is one of the leading advocates in the country for people with mental illness. As the brother of a sister who has schizophrenia, he shares our interest in this book.

Our book has profited considerably from the early support of Jeremy Tarcher and the assistance of two excellent editors, Lisa Chadwick and Mark Waldman. During the course of this book, I have been fortunate in having close colleagues at the University of Pittsburgh at Greensburg who have understood my mission, shared my enthusiasm, and provided ballast in heavy weather. With appreciation and affection, I mention Lillian Beeson, Rich Blevins, Mark McColloch, Frank McGlynn, Guy Rossetti, Norm Scanlon, and Judy Vollmer. I was also fortunate in having excellent undergraduate research and editorial assistants who worked on the book. These include Nelda Appleby, Pam Kowalczyk, Tom Kufashi, Shelli Labancz, John Lehner, Jami Leichliter, Jerilyn Lewis, Victoria McQuillis, Angel Murray, Mimi Owens, Susan Radvansky, Louann Stroud, Gwen Tharp, April Wateska, Janet Wilson, Nick Yackovich, and Nancy Young.

How to Cope with Mental Illness in Your Family is about families and about the losses and gains that accompany our most intimate relationships. As I was working on the book, I encountered both poles of the family experience due to the terminal illness of my mother, Anita Thimme. For more than fifty years, my life was sustained by her unwavering commitment to her children, her unflagging belief in our infinite potential, and her passion for life. Her death has truly left a chasm in my life; but far more, she has left a treasured heritage. At the core of that heritage are my sister, Meredith Kuhn, and my brothers, Jerry and Fred Thimme. Especially during this difficult period, I have cherished their presence in my life.

My life has been equally blessed by my own children and spouse: my three sons, Chris, Dan, and Steve, and my husband and personal pilot— in the air, on the sea, and in life—Rabe F. Marsh III.

DIANE T. MARSH
Greensburg, Pennsylvania

THE SIBLINGS AND OFFSPRING that we have noted have truly enriched my life. So, too, have the other members of NAMI that we have listed. My affiliation with Marylee Westbrook began when we both started our early support groups, and she continues to be a source of inspiration.

My early membership in NAMI was through the local chapter in Santa Barbara, CA. Joyce and Jerry Buck, Ann Eldridge, Frank Griscom, Nancy Johnson, and other members warmly took me under their wing.

Friends who become lifetime traveling companions are a treasure, and I would like to acknowledge a few: Sheila Anderson, Nick Bilyk, John Gould, Ted Heideman, Mike Majchrzak, Eric Mann, Carl Newman, Robert Rankin, and Julie Weiskircher.

Finally, part of who I am comes from my immediate family members, and I would like to recognize them: my deceased father, Donald, and brother, David; my mother, Maxine; and my siblings, John, Bruce, and Mary.

REX M. DICKENS
Hedrick, Iowa

INTRODUCTION

This mental illness business affected all aspects of my life—self-esteem, trust, intimacy, and hope. It was like a large cloud had moved over our heads and everyone was paralyzed for years. My parents were so consumed in their own drama that they had little energy or time for us children. I often felt as if I were in the middle of a game for which no one bothered to explain the rules. Gradually, I froze up emotionally. Life lost its color, and I lost my spontaneity and joy. REX M. DICKENS

THIS IS NOT a book about people with mental illness. Rather, it is a book about the family members who love them and have special challenges as a result. As you read this book, you'll learn about the impact of mental illness on your family, revisit the experiences of your childhood and adolescence, recognize the imprint of those experiences on your adult life, and learn how to cope more effectively in the present. You'll also find out about the unique concerns of siblings, of offspring, and of multigenerational family members, those who have both a sibling and a parent with mental illness.

Although we explore the impact of mental illness on all members of the family, our basic concern is young family members—those who have grown up with the mental illness of a parent or sibling. This early experience has a pervasive impact on your childhood and adolescence. It is also carried on to your adult life as a legacy that colors your view of the world and continues to influence your thoughts, feelings, and behavior. Reflecting our focus, we use the term *family members* to refer to siblings and offspring rather than other members of the family. We use the term *relative* to refer to the person in your family who has mental illness. Many other terms are used to refer to your relative, including *patient* or *client* (used by mental health professionals) and *consumer* or *survivor* (used by people with mental illness themselves).

The book was also written for those who care about you—your parents, your spouse or partner, your friends, and concerned mental health professionals. We hope they will find it helpful in understanding your experiences and in meeting your needs. In fact, we have offered suggestions for parents and professionals in the appendices. But our primary focus is on you and other siblings and offspring. As the following woman conveys, all of you have been deeply affected by the mental illness in your families:

> As a child, I tried desperately never to have a problem because our family had so many. So I became perfectionistic and hid my fears, concerns, and needs from everyone. On the outside, I always appeared strong and self-assured, able to handle anything. But I developed a lot of shame.

As you proceed through *How to Cope with Mental Illness in Your Family,* you'll hear from other family members who have shared your experience with mental illness. Over time—and with much heartache—they have learned how to cope with their family circumstances, to resolve their losses, and to move on with their lives. They have encountered many risks, challenges, and opportunities along the way, often emerging as better and stronger people. Their story is your story as well, one that embodies the most basic concerns about children and families.

These family members are reaching out to share their experiences and suggestions with you and to join with others who have been despondent over the mental illness of a beloved relative. They describe their experiences with power and eloquence, offering compelling witness to the impact of mental illness on their entire lives.

The voices of these family members came primarily from three sources: our national surveys of adult siblings and offspring; another book, *Anguished Voices,* that consists entirely of personal accounts by family members; and transcribed material from interviews, a panel presentation, and a support group. A few of the vignettes came from other sources, including our other research projects and chance encounters with family members who were willing to share their experiences with our readers. These are all real people. We made only a few changes in their actual words, using generic categories for proper names, such as a particular family member, professional, or place of treatment.

These family members have shared in your anguish, learned from their mistakes, and persisted in their effort to prevail over the adversity in their lives. Often, their progress is painfully slow; time and again it is thwarted by obstacles and reverses; and almost always it is accompanied by suffering. Still, there is much to learn from their frustrations, from their missteps, and from their triumphs. These family members can serve as your traveling companions, accompanying you on your journey of hope and healing. The following woman talks about the value of these companions in her own life:

The experience of being with others with similar experiences has been one of healthy validation. Only those who have experienced the catastrophe of mental illness in their families can fully understand the depth and breadth of emotions, the feeling of "wandering in the dark," trying to find an explanation for this illness. I did not have to feel ashamed or stigmatized. I was received by open minds and open hearts.

Together we, the authors, bring a wide range of experiences and expertise to the writing of *How to Cope with Mental Illness in Your Family,* though we arrived at this book from two very different paths. My professional path is that of a psychologist specializing in the area of serious mental illness. During the course of my contacts with parents, I began to hear from adult siblings and offspring, the millions of "forgotten family members" who had grown up with the mental illness of a sister, brother, mother, or father. Their voices conveyed a special vulnerability; their early experience with mental illness was woven into the very fabric of their souls. Over time, I came to enter their world, to share their grief, and to discover their wisdom. I resolved that their voices, too, would be heard. This book is the result of that commitment.

The other author is Rex Dickens, whose words appear at the beginning of this chapter. His personal account is contained in our book, *Anguished Voices*. His path to this book has been profoundly personal, for he has had to deal with the mental illness of his mother and three siblings. Like many family members, for many years Rex had little awareness of how much this had affected his life. It was only after his brother David's suicide that he began his own journey to come to terms with the mental illness in his family.

Over the years we have heard from countless family members. They have shared their stories with us and encouraged us to write a book for other siblings and offspring. We have also learned much from support groups for family members. Rex has spent years as a participant, organizer, and facilitator of such groups. We often hear that support groups serve as a life raft for family members, offering validation, information, comfort, and practical advice. These groups provide a protected forum for learning about mental illness, for developing essential coping skills, for resolving losses, and for sharing your journey with other family members. As one family member affirmed, "It helped me build a person out of the shell that I was."

We have also learned from our own research and from the research of others. For example, we conducted two national surveys of adult siblings and offspring, designed to explore their experience of mental illness. They identified their most important needs and coping resources during childhood, adolescence, and adulthood, and they also offered suggestions for family members and professionals. Another useful source has been the workshops we conduct for families and professionals. These workshops have provided an opportunity to learn from participants, to offer information and suggestions, and to assist family members in developing support groups and other services.

Finally, both of us are active on local, state, and national levels, working for a more humane and responsive system of care that can improve the lives of people affected by mental illness. We recognize that the family experience of mental illness is an intensely personal one, but we also feel you can benefit from increased understanding of the mental health system and the larger context in which it is embedded. Throughout this book we will share the insights we have gained from our personal experience and research. We hope you will find this information interesting and helpful.

THE SaC SYNDROME

Based on our contacts with family members, we are convinced that siblings and offspring have a unique set of experiences, needs, and difficulties. We have called this the SaC (Sibling and Child) Syndrome. An enormous number of people are affected by the SaC Syndrome. It is estimated that more than five million people in the United States have a serious mental illness. All of these people have family members—people who love them, who serve as a cornerstone of their support system, who often provide caregiving, and who suffer the losses that accompany the illness. Thus, far from being alone, you are part of a legion of family members who have shared your experiences, concerns, and challenges.

The SaC Syndrome is very large in another sense as well, for we are dealing with the most fundamental themes of human existence: the vulnerability of children, the risks of intimacy, the search for meaning and coherence, the complexity of family bonds, the fragility of the human mind, and the resilience of human beings. This is a book about people like you, whose lives have been forged in the caldron of mental illness. Through their sorrow, these family members have struggled to understand themselves and their families, to honor their commitment to their relatives, and to become better, stronger, and more tolerant people.

Thus, the SaC Syndrome covers a broad expanse of territory, a variety of family experiences, and numerous personal consequences, both positive and negative. Whatever their differences, however, family members almost universally describe a powerful struggle to maintain the integrity of their own lives in the wake of the mental illness in their families. In the words of one family member, "I continued to work toward my own self-preservation. I felt that I had to do whatever I could to salvage my own life."

The voices of the following family members illustrate some aspects of the SaC Syndrome. As a young child, this sibling tried to compensate her parents for the mental illness of her sister, minimizing her own needs in the process:

> I learned from a young age that I should act mature and self-reliant and not cause any waves. I did not want to hurt my parents after observing how much my sister had hurt them. I kept my difficulties to myself and kept up a good front in part

because I didn't want my parents to be disappointed. I finally sought counseling at the age of thirty.

The next family member has a parent and two siblings with mental illness. As her family life shattered, she felt compelled to remain strong and healthy, denying how she felt inside:

> For many years, my siblings and I had no real mother or father, no parent we could look to for comfort, strength, help— that sense of security. I felt that someone had to stay strong, and so, of course, I took on that role. I called it "the burden to be healthy." As a result, I hid my own pain, spending my time worrying about and trying to take care of everyone else.

Each of these women struggled to meet the needs of their distraught families at their own expense, and both of them developed impressive strengths in the process. Throughout *How to Cope with Mental Illness in Your Family,* we'll explore this common pattern and other dimensions of the SaC Syndrome. For example, we'll discuss:

- how your entire family is affected by the mental illness of your relative;

- the special risks, challenges, and opportunities confronting siblings, offspring, and multigenerational family members;

- the impact of your relative's mental illness on your own childhood and adolescence; and

- the legacy you have carried into your adult life.

We'll also assist you in using your new understanding to make constructive changes in your life. For example, you will learn how to:

- meet your needs as a family member;

- enhance your coping ability;

- develop a Personal Action Plan;

- deal with the mental health system; and
- improve your family relationships.

As you proceed through this book, you'll learn more about the SaC Syndrome and its meaning for your life. You'll also discover how to minimize the adverse effects of your early encounter with mental illness and to build on the strengths you've acquired.

What We Mean by Serious Mental Illness

Throughout the book we use the term *serious mental illness* to refer to the most severe and persistent mental disorders. These disorders include schizophrenia, major depression, manic depression (also called bipolar disorder), delusional disorder, panic disorder, obsessive-compulsive disorder, and other serious conditions. Our focus is on the first three disorders, which are among the most prevalent and disabling of the mental disorders. As with chronic medical conditions, these disorders have a profound impact on family members as well as their relatives.

These mental illnesses are serious because they can be extremely incapacitating and are often long-term. They are mental in the sense that they are brain disorders that affect all aspects of functioning, including thoughts, feelings, and behavior. And they are illnesses in much the same way that heart disease and cancer are illnesses. The difference is that serious mental illness affects the brain rather than the heart, lungs, or other body organs.

It is only in the past few decades that we have gained an understanding of the biological basis of serious mental illness and developed effective methods of treatment. In the past, these illnesses were poorly understood and, as a result, were often blamed on "dysfunctional families" or other nonbiological causes. But we now have a wealth of evidence that these disorders result from impairments in brain structure and chemistry. Similarly, we now have a wide array of effective treatments and programs for people with serious mental illness, who receive assistance in leading meaningful and productive lives in their communities. These constructive developments have also significantly improved the lives of their family members.

Let us briefly take a look at the three most serious disorders: schizophrenia, major depression, and manic depression.

Schizophrenia

Approximately 1 percent of the population suffers from schizophrenia—one out of every 100 people. Schizophrenia is characterized by a wide range of cognitive, social, behavioral, and emotional symptoms, as well as impairment in major areas of functioning, such as education, work, interpersonal relations, or self-care.

Professionals sometimes distinguish between the "positive" and "negative" symptoms of schizophrenia. Positive symptoms involve the *presence* of certain unusual experiences, thoughts, and feelings. These symptoms include:

- hallucinations (false perceptions), such as hearing voices;

- delusions (false beliefs), such as a conviction that one is being persecuted;

- disorganized thinking or speech; and

- bizarre behavior.

Negative symptoms involve an *absence* or decline of certain normal functions. Such symptoms may include:

- apathy and inability to follow through on tasks;

- inability to experience pleasure and to enjoy relationships;

- inability to feel and express emotions;

- inability to focus on activities; and

- impoverished thought and speech.

Approximately 10 percent of individuals with this disorder commit suicide. Schizophrenia appears most often in the early to mid-twenties for males and in the late twenties for females. For some individuals, the symptoms remain chronic or get worse, while for others they may improve. Complete remission is not common, although many individuals recover sufficiently to enjoy satisfying and productive lives. Of those who remain ill, some have a relatively stable course, whereas others will experience a more turbulent and debilitating path.

Major Depression

Major depression is an emotional disturbance that involves depressed mood and loss of interest or pleasure in nearly all activities. Additional symptoms may include:

- changes in appetite or weight, sleep, or activity level;

- decreased energy;

- feelings of worthlessness or guilt;

- difficulty thinking, concentrating, or making decisions; and

- recurrent thoughts of death or suicide.

Psychotic features may be present, such as delusions or hallucinations. Even in mild cases, it interferes significantly with life. In severe cases, the person may be unable to function socially or occupationally, or to perform minimal self-care activities like eating or dressing. Nearly 15 percent of individuals suffering with major depression commit suicide.

The disorder occurs twice as often among women and may begin at any time, often in the mid-twenties. Untreated, a major depression may last six months or longer. In most cases, the symptoms disappear and the person returns to a normal level of functioning. Some will experience complete recovery, others will have isolated episodes, and still others will experience more frequent episodes with age.

Manic Depression (Bipolar Disorder)

The symptoms of manic depression involve an abnormally and persistently elevated, euphoric, or irritable mood. Additional symptoms may include:

- inflated self-esteem or grandiosity (exaggerated self-importance);

- decreased need for sleep;

- increased talkativeness or pressure to keep talking;

- racing thoughts;

- distractibility (easily drawn to unimportant or irrelevant concerns);

- increased involvement in goal-directed activities or work;

- restlessness; and

- excessive involvement in potentially harmful activities, such as buying sprees, sexual indiscretions, or foolish business investments.

Psychotic features may also be present, including delusions or hallucinations. During a manic episode individuals may exhibit uncharacteristic, inappropriate, and bizarre behavior, as well as poor judgment and excessive activity. Suicide occurs in 10 percent to 15 percent of these individuals. Most people first experience a manic episode in their early twenties, but it can begin at any time, from adolescence to old age. Most individuals, however, will return to a fully functional level between episodes, and many experience both manic and depressive symptoms, with one episode following the other.

The Problem of Diagnosis

Although we focus on schizophrenia, major depression, and manic depression, this book is likely to be helpful for family members who are dealing with other mental health problems, because families are almost always affected when their relative has a mental disorder such as an eating disorder, an anxiety disorder, or a substance abuse disorder. In fact, these and other mental disorders may occur along with a serious mental illness. For instance, almost 50 percent of people with schizophrenia will also develop a substance abuse disorder at some point in their lives, and 25 percent will have an alcohol or drug abuse disorder at any given time.

In the beginning, it may be difficult to establish an accurate diagnosis, and family members may be given different diagnoses by various professionals. In some cases, professionals fail to communicate with family members and to inform them of their relative's diagnosis. In other cases, however, there may be genuine differences of opinion among professionals regarding the appropriate diagnosis. These differences can result in substantial frustration for family members. Needless to say, an absence of consensus regarding your relative's diagnosis can undermine his or her treatment and recovery.

In our research, we heard from family members who indicated they were uncertain about the nature of their relative's mental health problems, or who had lived with their relative's symptoms for many years before hearing a diagnosis. This uncertainty can occur if the symptoms were relatively brief and mild, the person refused to accept professional help, or families were not informed about the illness. Occasionally, family members recognize their relative's symptoms from magazine articles or television programs about mental illness, although others may remain in the dark about their relative's problems.

Family members who are dealing with a nameless disorder face special challenges. Under these circumstances, it is difficult to understand and cope with the symptoms of mental illness, to have a meaningful discussion with your other family members, or to arrive at reasonable expectations for yourself and your relative. Here is what happened to Rex:

> Mental health professionals ignored me. For years, David had been under their care. Not once had they ever told us what was wrong with him, what we could expect, or what would be helpful for us in dealing with him. I expected a cure, but there was none. I knew nothing, was told nothing, and thus did not know my expectation was unrealistic. This professional neglect of our family undermined our ability to understand and deal with his illness, with consequences that were devastating for us all.

A JOURNEY OF HOPE

It has been suggested that there are three essential elements of hope. First, hope requires a meaningful goal. We assume you are reading this book because you already have such a goal: coming to terms with the mental illness in your family. The second element is willpower: the reservoir of determination and commitment that drives us toward our goals. Again, if you are reading this book, you undoubtedly have the motivation to achieve your goal. What you and other family members are most often missing is the third element: waypower. Waypower is the pathways that guide us toward our goals—our mental maps or road plans. That is what we can provide in *How to Cope with Mental Illness in Your Family*.

We end this chapter by offering vignettes from the journeys of some of your traveling companions. All of them began their troubled journey many years ago, struggling to cope with a cataclysmic event that threatened to overwhelm their families. During the course of their lives, they have learned to deal with the mental illness in their own families, served as advocates for their relatives, and used their expertise to assist other family members.

The first family member is Linda Lattner, a sibling who lives in the Pittsburgh area. She was twenty when her brother was diagnosed with schizophrenia. Linda talks about its impact on her family:

> You're shocked and absolutely devastated. I felt an immediate deep sense of loss and went through a full array of emotions. I bargained with God. I was ashamed—there is so much stigma attached to mental illness. I felt guilty, wondering if there wasn't something more I could have done. I cried and wondered what was happening to us. Instantly, an entire family becomes paralyzed. My family and I withdrew—from each other, from our extended family, and from our neighbors. Nobody understood.

Many years later, Linda describes the strengths she and her family have developed through their encounter with mental illness:

> I've become a much stronger person. I'm far more compassionate and considerate toward others. I've become much

more philosophical. Our family learned exactly what we value, and I think it's brought us even closer to each other. I have really become appreciative and respectful of my own mental abilities. I thank God for another good day of rational thinking.

The second family member is Judy Flanigan, who grew up with a mother who had mental illness. She currently lives in New Jersey, although she spent many years in Pittsburgh, where she facilitated a support group with Linda. Judy recalls some of her early experiences:

> I had to be seven or eight. Dad would say, "You have to do things around the house to help Mother." I would have to do more and more; it seemed like Mother did less and less. I didn't grow up with affection and approval as a child. If you don't have those things, you don't know if you're a valuable person or not. I was insecure. I wondered what I had done wrong. I was so very, very sensitive. I wanted to be liked and loved by everyone.

Judy believes her involvement in support groups has been central to her own healing process. Members of her group heard her anguish, listened to her story, and reinforced her strengths:

> There is a need for somebody who really listens to you and can share your experiences and concerns. They would let me cry when I needed to cry. Every time I tell the story, the pain gets less. I've been through a lot. And those things in the past helped me go through the challenges of life. I have strong values and resilience. I'm a better person today.

The third fellow traveler is my coauthor Rex, a family member who has dealt with the mental illness of his mother, two brothers, and a sister. Like many family members, Rex initially fled his family, gaining as much geographical and psychological distance as possible. Ultimately, however, he realized he was carrying his legacy with him; it could not be jettisoned so easily. His real journey began following his brother David's suicide.

The central event of his life—the mental illness—could no longer be ignored.

At the time of his brother's death, Rex was a pilot for a commuter airline in California. He had returned from a day trip when he received a late-night call from one of his brothers informing him that David had shot himself. He describes his feelings at the time:

> It was too much. I cried uncontrollably for days. I cried for his tragedy, the tragedy of the others, the pain it was all causing me, the loss of our collective hopes and dreams, the horror of it all. Mental illness had created an emotional holocaust.

It has been over a decade since David's death. The intervening years have been challenging and productive. They have been marked by many changes, as Rex observes:

> I am learning to take care of myself; to give myself, personally, as much consideration as I give to others. I am becoming aware of my own emotional needs and wants. After years, decades actually, of being emotionally frozen, it is a joy to experience my reawakening.

After many difficult years, Linda, Judy, and Rex have all emerged from their past with a renewed sense of hope and satisfaction in the present. Each of them has heard the call to service, investing countless hours in supporting other family members. They have organized and facilitated support groups, served on the boards of family advocacy organizations, and offered workshops for other family members.

During one of Rex's workshops, he noticed one sibling who seemed upset by his presentation. Afterwards he approached her and said he was sorry if his comments had been too sad or painful for her. "Oh, no, no," she remarked, "it wasn't that. They were tears of joy because I was finally able to identify and connect together some pieces of my own experience." We trust you will share her enlightenment as you move through this book.

Chapter 1

YOUR JOURNEY OF
HOPE AND HEALING

❧

*My adolescent years were filled with a hollow dread. I felt some-
how that I was responsible. I felt incredibly angry, resentful toward my mother, unable to escape, and very guilty. Gradually I
have come to see my mother's mental illness as just one part of
my life. I have my own life, dreams, and goals. Her illness has
caused me to develop tremendous strength, discipline, and personal
stability.*

FROM THE VANTAGE POINT of midlife, this adult offspring of a
mother with mental illness relates her own journey. As her words
convey, the journey of family members is a troubled one; and it is
lifelong, with new issues, challenges, and opportunities at every stage. Yet
for all of her emotional turmoil, this woman has nevertheless managed to
place the mental illness in perspective—as a single event in her own life—
and to pursue her own hopes and dreams. As is the case for many family
members, she has also developed some impressive personal qualities
along the way.

This book involves another journey, one that can assist you in coming
to terms with the mental illness in your family and in sharing the triumphs of this family member. At the center of this journey is a process of
naming and taming.

So often the family experience of mental illness is shrouded in secrecy, hidden from the outside world, and concealed from the well children in the family. As a result, you may have grown up frightened about your relative's symptoms and confused by your family's repeated crises. Perhaps you accepted some responsibility for these events. Along with other members of your family, you may have internalized the stigma surrounding mental illness as something wrong with you. All of these problems are heightened when the mental illness is not discussed openly within the family. And when it is not named, the mental illness cannot be tamed.

On a recent Father's Day, on the anniversary of her father's suicide a decade earlier, a woman wrote about his mental illness in *The Washington Post*. She described the disintegration of her family and their periodic descent into an "evil parallel universe of surreal, episodic madness." But it was not the madness that caused the greatest harm. It was her family's failure to name and tame:

> I heard too much and I saw too much but it was the total lack
> of acknowledgment that I had in fact seen or heard anything
> that ultimately warped me. Our family code of silence care-
> fully preserved our illusory outer shell, but that silence caused
> me to grow internally misshapen, flawed.

This book offers you an opportunity to name and tame the aftershocks of mental illness in your own life—the pattern we have called the Sibling and Child Syndrome, or SaC Syndrome for short. With each leg of your journey, you'll shine a light on your shadowy past, learn the universal dimensions of your personal journey, and resolve some of your earlier losses. This process of naming and taming will strip the illness of its power over your life and release your energy for the present.

Your naming and taming of the SaC Syndrome will occur throughout *How to Cope with Mental Illness in Your Family*. This journey of hope and healing has landmarks, legs, and mileposts. Let's take a closer look.

LANDMARKS

Landmarks are the experiences and events that mark each leg of your journey. As with any journey, they include the backdrop of sights and sounds, the major paths and byways, the road signs and signals, the hazards and obstacles along your route, and your chance encounters with other travelers.

Some landmarks are unique to your particular journey as a family member. For example, as a consequence of the mental illness in your family, you are likely to encounter:

- a set of unique experiences, concerns, and challenges;
- a family legacy that shadows your own life;
- a personal legacy that influences your thoughts, feelings, and behavior; and
- an interpersonal legacy that affects your relationships inside and outside your family.

As you can see, some of the important landmarks pertain to your family's experience of mental illness. Others etch your own course through childhood, adolescence, and adulthood. Still others involve your relationships and your process of coming to terms with the illness. Together, these landmarks define the SaC Syndrome.

Chances are you'll recognize only some of the landmarks described in this book, since each journey is a very personal one. Familiar landmarks will probably evoke a sense of having traveled this route before, of having encountered these places, events, and people on an earlier trip. As you proceed, you'll have an opportunity to reencounter the past in a new way—with courage and confidence rather than your earlier trepidation and doubt. You'll also be able to chart your progress, as you pass some landmarks, pause at others, and anticipate those on a future leg.

One common landmark is the powerful sense of responsibility so often experienced by family members. Especially when you were younger, you may have felt compelled to hold your shaken family together, to meet the needs of your other family members at your own expense, or even to "rescue" your relative. Witnessing this cataclysmic family event, possibly you developed a strong sense of responsibility on your own. Or perhaps others inside or outside your family implored you to shoulder an oversized portion of your family's burden. In either case, you faced an unmanageable task—no child is prepared to assume adult responsibilities.

The landmark of personal responsibility may appear on many legs of your journey. The following woman conveys the distress young family members may experience when forced to assume responsibilities for which they are unprepared:

> I was forced to deal with "grown-up" problems. No one was taking care of me. I had a great deal of difficulty understanding and explaining to friends why my mother had "nervous breakdowns." I cried myself to sleep at night. I had no one to talk to. I never felt that it was acceptable to cry or talk about it. I accepted a great deal of responsibility in trying to help my father out.

LEGS

Legs are the six stages in your journey of hope and healing. These include:

- revisiting your childhood;
- reclaiming your childhood;
- reflecting on your current life;
- resolving your legacy;
- revising your legacy; and
- renewing your life.

The legs of your journey unfold in a natural sequence. Each leg has its recognizable landmarks and mileposts, and each lays the foundation for a subsequent leg. But this journey does not have a straightforward course; nor does it have a final destination. Rather, the journey is circular and cyclical, meandering and returning you again and again to earlier stages and issues. These repeated encounters allow you to approach prior problems in new ways and with better results. In some respects it is like walking through a woodland and stepping from time to time into a stream that winds along your path. You reenter the same stream, but further along and with a fresh perspective.

Likewise, unlike many other journeys, this one involves a process rather than a destination. Your feelings of grief and loss are never fully resolved. In fact, your painful feelings may be experienced for a lifetime, waxing and waning to the rhythms of your life. Old issues and concerns may resurface with intensity at any time, perhaps in response to a crisis in your family or to difficulties in your own life. That doesn't mean there is no progress, only that your journey is likely to be uneven, with reverses as well as gains.

Your journey needs to unfold at its own pace—it cannot be rushed. Each family member will find a comfortable tempo for acknowledging important landmarks, completing the essential legs, and achieving significant mileposts. Be patient with yourself and with your other family members. In a real sense, this journey is never fully completed. But as each sunrise offers the promise of a new day, each leg of your journey offers hope for a better tomorrow.

As with your journey through life, each stage leaves its imprint. Earlier experiences and events are carried on as memories, images, thoughts, and feelings that echo through each succeeding stage, influencing your behavior, choices, and relationships. Sometimes this imprint involves a legacy of unfinished business—of unmet needs, of incomplete tasks, of unfinished conversations, of unresolved conflicts—that can slow or even interrupt your journey. We hope our book will help you complete some of this unfinished business and move on to the next leg in your journey.

MILEPOSTS

Mileposts mark the significant turning points between legs. They are major accomplishments that offer:

- a sense of completion and satisfaction;

- an opportunity to pause and rest;

- an occasion to review your progress; and

- a chance to prepare for the next leg.

Unlike landmarks, which may be very personal, important mileposts are usually shared by all members of your family. For each of you, important mileposts are reached when you are able to accept the illness, to understand the personal meaning of the illness, to resolve your losses, to renew family relationships, and to reinvest in your present life.

Although they are often shared, mileposts are achieved in unique ways and at different times by members of the same family. This can be cause for conflict and confusion, especially if some members continue to deny or minimize the illness. Accepting the reality of mental illness is enormously difficult for family members and for their relatives, who often say acceptance was among the most formidable challenges of their lives.

As a result, some members may remain caught in a web of denial or disbelief that prevents them from reaching the milepost of acceptance and adapting with the rest of the family. In other families, mutual acceptance allows members to work together in coping with daily problems and in planning for the future.

Ultimately, however, your own journey is deeply personal, with its own prominent landmarks, its own rhythm and pace, its special guides and companions. The following sibling talks about her own painful process of reaching acceptance. Once she reached this milepost, her pain began to diminish:

> The first five years of her illness were a nightmare for me. I couldn't accept that the illness was permanent, that my sister couldn't pull herself out of it. I couldn't accept the loss of my "real" sister. I slowly came to accept my sister's illness. With this acceptance, the pain and grief I felt disappeared.

CONFRONTING THE PAST

Whatever our differences, all of us have encountered psychological mines in the past—people, experiences, or events that represent special threats. As with the weapons of war, these psychological mines are small fireworks that may scatter with a loud retort. The fragments—or shrapnel— of these mines constitute the unfinished business of our lives. This shrapnel becomes embedded in our psyches, reverberating through the years to come.

As with real shrapnel, we need to know more before proceeding: where the fragments are located, as well as their nature and potential for further damage. Some fragments are best left in place, either because they are harmless or because their removal exacts an unacceptable cost. Other fragments carry uncertain risks, which can be dealt with as necessary. Still others require a rapid response because of their actual or potential harm. In the same way, our psychological shrapnel requires further inspection. Some fragments are best left alone; others can be monitored for possible future action. But some unfinished business demands our immediate attention.

This approach is similar to the triage process that governs the treatment of battle and disaster victims. Medical personnel direct their efforts toward helping those who are most likely to benefit from treatment, making best use of limited resources. A triage process can also assist you in allocating your finite emotional energy. No one ever completes all the unfinished business of the past or fully resolves the inevitable losses of life. It is enough to target those fragments with the greatest potential for harm and for change.

Our goal is to assist you in applying a triage process to your unfinished business. We'll assist you in understanding the SaC Syndrome, identifying your psychological mines, and defusing some of the shrapnel. This is a hopeful process that affords you an opportunity to revisit and reclaim your past and to enrich your present.

This process represents an investment in your future that requires both time and energy and that carries potential gains as well as risks. We'll take a look at both possibilities.

POTENTIAL BENEFITS

Revisiting your past offers many potential gains. These include an opportunity to obtain:

- validation of your personal experiences;
- greater insight and understanding;
- resolution of earlier issues and losses; and
- increased satisfaction in the present.

Validation of your encounter with mental illness occurs as you name and tame the SaC Syndrome. You'll learn about the universal dimensions of your personal experience and join the community of those who have shared your journey. You will also gain greater understanding of mental illness, your family, and yourself. Your new knowledge will enable you to reframe your legacy as a normal response to an abnormal family event.

With validation and understanding comes an opportunity for resolution—completion of important unfinished business—and for making constructive changes in your life. Less of your energy will be drained away. Building on these accomplishments, you may achieve greater self-acceptance and inner peace, make new choices in important areas of your life, and improve your relationships inside and outside your family.

The following woman describes many of these benefits for herself and her family. After many difficult years, she and her family members gathered to explore the meaning of the mental illness in their midst. Here is her description of their encounter:

> Our family met for a weekend to discuss my brother's illness and its impact on our family. The meeting included the five siblings and their spouses, as well as our parents. We broke down a lot of barriers. There was a lot of laughing, a lot of crying, and a lot of anger. We're learning to be more honest with each other. It helped us to get out of our various roles and to relate to one another as adults. After the meeting, we felt truly closer.

Potential Risks

All journeys—whether geographical or psychological—involve some risks. Because you are required to revisit painful emotional territory, this particular journey carries some special risks. For example, your journey may:

- undermine familiar—but maladaptive—coping strategies;

- release painful feelings, images, and memories;

- temporarily increase your distress; and

- expose you to emotional flooding.

When faced with threatening situations, we have two choices. We can attempt to shut down and avoid these situations, a strategy that offers protection but prevents us from coping. Or we can open up and confront them, which increases our vulnerability but allows us to move on. Many family members have opted for avoidance in the past, largely because of their youth. To protect yourself as a child, you may have partially cut off painful memories, images, or feelings. This splitting off of part of your mind is called dissociation.

Possibly you attempted to shut down your emotional life altogether, a process called psychic numbing. As an adult, you may pay a high price for this earlier protection, losing touch with portions of your inner life and remaining imprisoned in an emotional desert. Strategies based on avoidance may have helped you survive in the past, but they have become maladaptive in the present. In the words of one family member, "I put so much energy into squelching my feelings that I eventually lost touch with them entirely."

In contrast, the process of naming and taming requires an honest and direct confrontation with your past. As you learn to deal with your past more openly, your earlier avoidance strategies are weakened, which may result in the release of painful feelings, images, and memories that have built up over many years. Existing below the surface, these feelings may reappear forcefully and unexpectedly. This process is sometimes called emotional flooding. When these powerful emotions are unleashed, it may seem as if a dam has broken, leaving you feeling anxious and overwhelmed. Revisiting your painful childhood, as you are doing in this book, may increase this risk and temporarily intensify your distress. This is the price you are willing to pay for a more fulfilling future.

There is also another source of emotional flooding—the shock of recognition you may feel after so many years of struggling alone. It can be unsettling to learn that your personal experiences are shared by so many other family members. Yet learning that your powerful feelings are a normal and natural response to an abnormal family event is essential to your healing process.

You can approach the risk of emotional flooding in a number of ways. It helps to anticipate the possibility of this risk and to understand its sources. In addition, you can structure the process to avoid or minimize the risk of emotional flooding. You can also be prepared if it does happen.

When to Seek Professional Counseling

Personal counseling offers a valuable resource for some family members. In fact, three-quarters of family members who responded to our surveys indicated they had received counseling themselves. The level was even higher among multigenerational family members and those who were age ten or younger at the onset of their relative's mental illness. Almost all of these family members found counseling helpful.

Counseling can assist you in understanding and lessening the symptoms of the SaC Syndrome or in dealing with other problems that may have been aggravated by the stress in your family. For most family members, counseling is simply an option that can offer comfort and guidance in stormy weather. However, professional assistance is more of a necessity for some family members, including those who suffer from any of the following:

- severe and persistent depression;

- sharp mood swings;

- severe anxiety, panic, or fear;

- abuse of alcohol or drugs; or

- significant health or physical problems without an underlying cause.

If you are unsure whether to seek personal counseling, it may be helpful to obtain a consultation from a mental health professional, such as a psychiatrist, psychologist, social worker, family therapist, or counselor. Your consultation can help you clarify your concerns and decide whether counseling is likely to be helpful. Later we'll discuss counseling in more detail.

STRATEGIES FOR USING THIS BOOK

Here are some strategies that can assist you in obtaining maximum gain from *How to Cope with Mental Illness in Your Family*. They may help you avoid or minimize emotional flooding, digest the material in the book, and apply it to your own life.

Pacing

You are likely to benefit most from your journey of hope and healing if you establish a comfortable pace. Begin by scanning the table of contents to get a sense of the entire journey. Then read a chapter at a time, pausing between chapters to review the material or to discuss it with others. If you experience some emotional flooding, limit your reading to a few sections at a time.

Taking a Time-Out

If things get too intense, take a time-out. A break can give you a chance to to reflect on the material, to see how it relates to your life, and to regain your perspective. When you return to the book, you'll probably find it less stressful and more meaningful.

Shifting to the Present

As we've observed, revisiting your past can evoke painful feelings. If your visit becomes uncomfortable, simply shift to the present. Take a walk, call a friend, attend a film or a concert, or turn to another pleasurable activity.

Remember, your goal is to enrich your present, not to remain trapped in your past.

Seeking Support

While you are coming to terms with your painful past, you need to strengthen your own support network. Spend time with treasured friends and develop new friendships. Other people are your most important resource.

Sharing the Journey

Family members often cite the benefits of their participation in a specialized support group for adult siblings and offspring. Chances are a family support group is available in your community, but its membership may consist largely of parents whose adult sons or daughters have mental illness. You can locate your nearest group for siblings and offspring by calling your local or state chapter of the National Alliance for the Mentally Ill (you can get these numbers by contacting NAMI; see Appendix A).

Working Through the Issues

Certain activities can help you work through the issues discussed in the book. For example, you may find it useful to keep a journal, recording your reactions or the points you want to remember. Or you may prefer to direct your insights into art, music, or drama. These expressive channels offer an alternative to our usual verbal modes of reading, writing, and talking with others.

Increasing Your Knowledge

This book offers a wealth of information about mental illness, the family experience of the illness, the SaC Syndrome, effective coping strategies, and the mental health system. You may wish to increase your knowledge of these or other topics. Many resources are listed in Appendix A. Local classes or workshops may also be helpful.

Improving Your Stress Management

Living with mental illness in the family is often extremely stressful. Undertaking this journey of hope and healing may also increase your level of stress, especially during the early legs, when you are reentering painful territory. Many strategies are available for stress reduction, including relaxation training, imagery, and meditation. Consider taking a stress-management workshop or pursuing a self-help program.

Expanding Your Boundaries

When asked for advice, many family members emphasize the importance of not letting the mental illness take over their lives. You can follow their counsel by increasing your activities and relationships outside your family. At the same time, your journey of hope and healing is likely to shrink your SaC Syndrome, releasing your energy for other pursuits.

Practicing Good Self-Care

Perhaps most important, you need to take good care of yourself. Many family members grow up minimizing their own needs. If you have neglected your needs in the past, undertake a program to improve your self-care. Maintain a comfortable balance in your life that includes sufficient sleep, proper nutrition, regular exercise, fulfilling relationships, and productive activities. Over the long term, a program of good self-care will improve your mental and physical health, enhance your stress management, and increase your satisfaction with life.

THE SIX LEGS OF THE JOURNEY

There are six legs in your journey of hope and healing. We'll explore each of these legs in the remaining chapters. Here we offer a brief overview that can prepare you for the journey to follow.

Revisiting Your Childhood

The first leg involves revisiting your childhood to learn about the impact of mental illness on your early years. You will return to the past not to remain there or to eclipse your present life, but to gain validation, insight, and understanding. This leg will help you counter the denial or distortion of the past and understand the impact of mental illness on your family.

As we'll discuss in the next chapter, mental illness affects all aspects of family functioning and all roles and relationships within the family. In the words of one family member, "An emotional sinkhole opened up within the family that no one seemed to understand." Listen as the following woman describes the impact of mental illness on her family:

> Mental illness is a ravaging, devastating disease that disrupts a family. I remember my mother crying a lot, being hostile, and family members trying to convince her to go to the hospital. It is a financial strain on the family and disrupts interpersonal relationships. It often isolates the family because of the stigma and the family member's inappropriate social behavior.

Reclaiming Your Childhood

During the second leg of your journey, you'll gradually reclaim your childhood as you learn how the mental illness affected your feelings about yourself, as well as your relationships inside and outside your family. In the past, you may have been largely unaware of the impact of the illness on your own life. This leg allows you to illuminate the dark recesses of your past and and to understand the personal meaning of mental illness.

Because you were exposed to mental illness as you were growing up, you share a special vulnerability with other siblings and offspring. Your earlier losses may have been enormous, perhaps even including the loss of childhood itself. As one family member has expressed it, "I feel like I missed out on being a kid."

In describing the impact of her father's mental illness on her early years, this woman conveys the particular vulnerability of young family members:

By the time I went to kindergarten, I was fearful and had lost my spontaneity. I had no energy to put into schoolwork. I felt helpless and inferior to the other children. I didn't want to bring the other kids to my house. I tried to always please my mom and make her happy. I became more and more focused on her life and neglected my own.

Reflecting on Your Current Life

The third leg of your journey focuses on your current life. As you shift from the past to the present, you'll learn how your relative's illness continues to influence your life and to impregnate your thoughts, feelings, and behavior. In the words of one family member, "My mother's illness shaped my life." You'll also see how old wounds can surface, often without your awareness.

The next family member has learned much about the personal meaning of mental illness. As in the case of so many family members, her early years left a harmful residue that infected her entire life:

> For many years I thought that no one would really want me because I came from a "defective" family. So I married someone who didn't appreciate me, and then embarked on a series of shallow relationships based on sex. I still have a tendency to hold back in relationships for fear that I will be abandoned. Somehow I still feel like that little girl who had to take care of everything herself.

Resolving Your Legacy

The fourth leg offers an opportunity to move beyond understanding and to achieve resolution. You'll discover the different phases of your adaptation process. You'll also learn about your needs as a family member and about the ways you can meet your needs. In naming and taming your outgrown maladaptive patterns, you can decide what works and what doesn't work. Then you can make new choices in the present.

As you name and tame your painful experiences, they will lose some of their control over your life. But earlier losses are never fully resolved;

they will always cast a shadow. As one family member has observed, "For many of us, the effects will continue for years to come. However, just knowing they exist makes them easier to battle."

The following multigenerational family member has fought and won many battles along the way:

> I'll fight the next battles successfully as well—accepting my mother for who she is now, not worrying about becoming ill myself, setting better boundaries between my family and me. The trouble is, I see life as a battlefield. With this tendency to look for and expect the worst, I go through life wearing a suit of armor. That way, when the worst hits, I'm ready for the blow. It's a hard way to live, though, encased in armor. I'm working on it—taking it off—piece by piece.

Revising Your Legacy

The fifth leg involves revising your legacy. By the end of this leg, your family experience of mental illness is no longer the major force in your life. It has been placed in perspective, as a single event in your life. Revising your legacy allows you to change the way you feel about the past. New perspectives and insights bring opportunities for change. Although you can't alter the past, you can modify its impact on the present.

Still, although your SaC Syndrome has faded into the background, it continues to flicker at the edge of your consciousness and may burst into flames with little warning—producing an emotional firestorm that undermines your equilibrium and briefly returns you to a more painful past. But you are no longer hostage to the past.

For several decades, the next family member felt that he was "buried alive" as a result of the SaC Syndrome. With assistance from members of his support group, he now envisions himself as a seed planted in difficult soil that is beginning to emerge from his "buried" years:

> The group helped transform my resentment toward my brother into understanding and compassion. I am now more accepting of myself and others and less dominated by strong negative emotions. Able to do things more effectively, I feel

more confident, less burdened with family issues, and more at peace and in touch with my true nature, goals, dreams, and passions.

Renewing Your Life

By the final leg of your journey, you'll have recaptured most of your energy, releasing it for your present life. You may also have gained more control over your feelings, thoughts, and behavior, and developed more confidence in your ability to cope with your family circumstances. We hope your past will recede to a degree that allows you to savor the present. Like many family members, you may even discover some unexpected benefits. For example, one sibling remarked that her challenges had made "the experience of living all the more rich."

Having gained a new perspective on your own life, you may wish to turn outward, reconnecting with your family and perhaps reaching out to other siblings and offspring. As your journey draws to a close, you may share the personal gains of the following woman. She has especially benefited from her contacts with other family members:

> Until recently, I had never discussed how growing up with a mentally ill parent had affected me. For years, I wasn't even aware of the effects. After two decades, I am finally discussing it. Not only with my siblings, but with others who grew up in homes similar to ours. We compare memories, express feelings, and admit fears. It crumbles the wall of isolation, it demystifies the illness, and most important of all, it validates who we are and why.

Your relative may also join in this recovery process, which is cause for celebration among all members of the family. The following family member has participated both in her brother's hardships and in his accomplishments:

> My brother's involuntary commitment and subsequent hospitalization were very stressful for my family. Don't give up hope. Given his original prognosis, his recovery has been just

short of miraculous. Although this could change, the future looks very bright. He still receives medication, lives quietly on his own, and holds a full-time job again.

We can't guarantee that your family will share in all of these positive outcomes. But, as this sibling implores, don't give up hope. Whatever your personal circumstances, you have the opportunity to transform your early suffering into insight, compassion, and resilience.

Chapter 2

REVISITING YOUR
CHILDHOOD

☙

*All family members are affected by a loved one's mental illness.
The entire family system needs to be addressed, to assure us that we
are not to blame and the situation is not hopeless, to point us to
people and places that can help our loved one. I was not informed
by anyone what my mother actually suffered from. I endured a lot
of unnecessary emotional pain. The impact still lingers on.*

A S   T H I S   F A M I L Y   member attests, mental illness wounds all
members of the family. And all carry scars from their encounter
with this unwelcome intruder. On this leg of your journey, we'll
revisit your childhood to explore the impact of mental illness on your
family as a unit and on your individual family members.

There are many catastrophic events that can traumatize families.
Some of these are natural disasters, such as earthquakes, floods, and tor-
nadoes. Others are unnatural disasters, such as war, poverty, and discrimination. More personal disasters include bereavement, divorce, and sexual
abuse. The mental illness of a close relative shares many characteristics
with these and other catastrophic events. But mental illness is unique in
some important ways.

Unlike other time-limited disasters, this one is woven into the lives of
individuals and families on a continuing basis; unlike those disasters that
result from environmental conditions, mental illness is profoundly per-

sonal; and unlike other personal disasters that have perpetrators who can be held accountable, mental illness involves someone else who is also victimized and traumatized. Moreover, unlike many other calamities, there is little social validation and support, and mental illness brings with it a corrosive stigmatization that often isolates and alienates family members. In this chapter, we'll take a closer look at this unique family event.

LANDMARKS

This leg of your journey includes three major landmarks. The first is the impact of your relative's mental illness on your family as a whole—your family system. As you'll see, the illness affects all members of your family, all areas of family functioning, and all family relationships.

Second, we'll examine some of the universal dimensions of your family's encounter with mental illness, including their experience of family burden, the risks that beset families, and their potential for a resilient response to this catastrophic event.

Third, we'll take a look at the impact of mental illness on individual members of your family, including your relative, your parents, and your well siblings. Each family member has particular experiences, needs, and concerns. And because all family members are connected, each of their experiences has implications for you.

HOW MENTAL ILLNESS DISRUPTS THE FAMILY

As we all know, families are changing along with society in general. We now have more two-career families with the increase of women in the work force, more blended families following the remarriage of divorced parents, and more single-parent families, including those headed by teenagers, fathers, and grandparents. Yet all families fulfill some basic functions. Some of the most important are:

- ensuring survival of their family members;
- providing for their safety and security;
- meeting their emotional and educational needs;

- coping with crisis;

- advocating for members; and

- fostering individual and family development.

Mental illness often interferes with a family's ability to fulfill these functions—not because your family was a "dysfunctional" one, but because mental illness is a catastrophic event. Your family operates like a kind of giant shock absorber that responds to events inside and outside the family. When these events strain the capacity of your family, their ability to perform their functions may be undermined.

At the most basic level, families need to assure the survival of their members and to provide for their safety and security. Thus, they require sufficient income to furnish food, clothing, shelter, and health care, as well as a safe and secure home environment. Most families are able to fulfill these essential survival functions in spite of the mental illness. But there are some exceptions, including families who are living in poverty, whose main wage earner develops the illness, who are living with the threat of violence, or who face problems in many areas of their lives.

The remaining family functions are almost always negatively affected by the mental illness of a close relative, which acts as a sinkhole that consumes family energy. Especially at the onset of the illness, individually and collectively family members may have few reserves to meet the emotional needs of others, to offer support and companionship, or to engage in recreation and leisure activities. When these functions cannot be fulfilled, your family's quality of life may be eroded.

So may the ability of your family to perform its educational function. Adult members of the family may be less available to teach young children social and academic skills. Teenagers may obtain little support in formulating appropriate career goals or in translating those goals into reality. Likewise, because of the stigma that encircles mental illness, families may find themselves cut off from important sources of information outside the family. For all of these reasons, as a child and adolescent you may have felt insecure about your social and academic skills and uncertain about your career plans.

As the mental illness continues to drain the family's energy, members may have difficulty coping with other crises, advocating for individual members, and encouraging their development. Especially during crises, all families experience some difficulty fulfilling their functions. Still, families vary in their response to mental illness and in their ability to fulfill their functions.

With time most families adapt to the illness and regain their ability to meet the needs of their members. One woman wrote about her family: "As terrible as it has been, I have gained a great sense of love and admiration for my family. We support one another through discussion, problem-solving, and humor." Yet some families have difficulty fulfilling their most basic functions, as the following family member attests: "Mother's illness had a profound effect. Safety, security, and trust were shattered. I was very scared and very confused."

The disruptive force of mental illness is often referred to as family burden. This burden has a subjective component, which consists of the emotional consequences of the illness for other family members, and an objective component, which consists of the practical problems that accompany mental illness.

THE SUBJECTIVE BURDEN

The emotional burden experienced by family members can leave them reeling and worried about their own mental health. In the words of one family member, "You feel angry, guilty, embarrassed, ashamed, confused, saddened, helpless, and hopeless. There is unprocessed grief, anxiety, resentment, preoccupation, self-doubt, and isolation." Another wrote: "There is a pain inside me that cannot be quelled." As a sibling or child of someone with mental illness, you are likely to experience:

- a sense of grief and loss for your relative, your family, and yourself;

- chronic sorrow as the illness is woven into your life on a continuing basis;

- an emotional roller coaster in response to the course of the disorder; and

- empathic pain as you share in your relative's and family's suffering.

Grief and Loss

At the core of the family experience of mental illness is a grieving process that was reported by 63 percent of our survey participants. Family members may mourn for the relative they have known and loved before the onset of the illness, for the anguish of their family, and for their own losses. Speaking for many others, one family member wrote about "losing my father to a living death."

Although the family experiences of biological death and mental illness differ in some important respects, the wake created by both events leaves family members profoundly shaken and bereft. One difference is that families who are dealing with biological death benefit from social validation and support. All of the rituals surrounding a death assist families in accepting the loss of their relative, in working through their grief, and in moving on in their lives.

In the case of mental illness, social validation and support are largely absent, leaving family members isolated and alienated. Especially if you experienced mental illness as a child, your grief may have remained unresolved. One woman wrote about her family's failure to acknowledge "that I really lost my mother even though she wasn't 'dead.' I never really got to express my grief until she died forty-six years later."

This complicated grieving process often subjects family members to a wide range of negative emotions, including shock, disbelief, grief, anger, guilt, and despair. Like many family members, you may have discounted your own grief, with harmful consequences for your later life. Here are the words of a multigenerational family member: "I tried to ignore my grief and help my parents and other siblings. I am still working on my pain, even though decades have passed."

Family members experience many losses, including symbolic losses that pertain to hopes, dreams, and expectations, and to individual and family myths and identity. For instance, family members may experience the loss of a "normal" family, perhaps finding themselves labeled "dysfunctional" simply because they have a relative with mental illness.

In addition to these losses, as a young family member you may be subject to the loss of childhood itself. One family member wrote about "my loss of a healthy mother, a normal childhood, and a stable home." Likewise, because your encounter with mental illness occurred before your personality had fully developed, your losses may have been assimilated into your emerging sense of yourself, as in the case of the following woman:

> I lost a sense of knowing who I am and of what I wanted. I lost the ability to set my own agenda and to control my own life. I lost sight of my own needs. I lost self-confidence. I lost the ability to care for myself properly. I feel out of sync with the normal developmental rhythms. I have been saddened in a chronic way.

Chronic Sorrow

Although many family members do experience a mourning process in response to their relative's mental illness, rarely do they move through a series of stages that culminate in a final state of peaceful acceptance. You are far more likely to experience continuing feelings of grief and loss that wax and wane in response to the course of your relative's illness or to events in your own life. These powerful emotions are woven into the familial fabric on a continuing basis, with the potential for periodic emotional firestorms. The following family member conveys this sense of chronic sorrow, which was noted by 64 percent of our participants: "It's like someone close died. But there's no closure. It's never over."

Emotional Roller Coaster

Family members sometimes say they feel they are riding an emotional roller coaster, punctuated by alternate periods of relapse and remission. But the periods of calm often provide little respite, imbued as they are with a sense of impending doom. In response to this unpredictability, families may remain in a state of vigilance, awaiting the next crisis. These cycles create considerable stress for family members, who often experience intense distress when renewed hope is shattered by yet another relapse. Here are the words of a sibling:

> It's like being on a roller coaster, going up or down. When my brother is okay, I'm up; when he's in the hospital, I'm down. It's devastating to any family—seeing my brother in a psychiatric unit of a hospital.

Empathic Pain

As family members begin to resolve their emotional burden, they often continue to experience empathic pain for the losses experienced by other family members, especially their relative. Indeed, empathic pain may remain insistent over time, as family members share in their relative's anguish over an impoverished life and in his or her struggle against the forces of psychosis. The empathic suffering of family members may strip their own lives of pleasure if they are subject to "survivor's guilt" that undermines their satisfaction with their accomplishments. One family member wrote about her own experience of empathic pain, "seeing the torment my brother and mother lived with every day and being helpless to do anything about it." Another talked about the difficulty of detaching himself from his mother's mental illness, "feeling as if her pain were my pain."

THE OBJECTIVE BURDEN

In addition to this powerful subjective burden, family members are confronted with an objective burden—the daily problems and challenges that accompany the mental illness. These include:

- symptoms of the illness, such as bizarre or frightening behavior;
- caregiving responsibilities for your relative;
- limitations of the mental health system; and
- social stigma, which continues to surround serious mental illness.

Symptoms

Family members often experience considerable distress in response to the symptoms of serious mental illness. As we noted earlier, symptoms of mental illness may include:

- positive symptoms, such as hallucinations, delusions, disorganized thought and speech, and bizarre behavior;

- negative symptoms, which involve a decline in normal experiences, thoughts, and feelings;

- disturbances of mood, including severely depressed mood, unusually elevated mood, or extreme mood swings;

- potentially harmful or self-destructive behavior;

- socially inappropriate or disruptive behavior; and

- poor daily living habits.

Certainly, people with mental illness are the greatest victims of these symptoms, which can adversely affect all aspects of their lives. Family members are also victimized by the symptoms of mental illness, either directly when they are the target of symptomatic behavior, or indirectly when they are helpless observers of their relative's aberrant behavior. The following man talks about the consequences of his father's illness for his own life:

> My father's paranoid schizophrenia meant we moved frequently, because he felt the conspiracy was closing in on him. He battered my mother, because he felt she was part of the conspiracy. I was too frightened to go to her aid. I couldn't have friendships with peers because my father felt they might "poison" my mind against him.

As in the case of this family member, you may have worried about the risk of violent or self-destructive behavior, as did more than half of our participants. Most people with mental illness are not dangerous, although they are often portrayed as such by the mass media. More than three-fourths of prime-time television portrayals of people with mental illness depict dangerous behavior, in contrast to an actual incidence of 3 percent.

But the specter of harm is very real for many family members. In fact, the death rate from suicide and other causes of death is significantly higher among individuals who have mental illness. According to some studies, the rate of suicide is between 10 percent and 15 percent for people who have schizophrenia, major depression, and manic depression. For certain family members, these statistics are translated into a terrible reality:

I feel an overwhelming sense of loss and tragedy. My father had his first major episode when I was eight years old. He died when I was seventeen. My brother had become ill two years earlier. When I was thirty-two, my brother died. He was hit by a drunk driver. I had another brother who committed suicide when he was twenty-seven. Thinking of either of my brothers or my father makes it difficult sometimes to want to continue living my own life.

Caregiving

Our present system of mental health care is fraught with difficulties. Family members often pay the price for inadequate community care, for the cracks in the system, and for the revolving hospital door that often returns patients to their families and their communities in a state of partial remission. As a result, families now fulfill crucial roles as primary caregivers for relatives who reside at home, as informal case managers, who advocate for their relatives with service providers, and as crisis intervention specialists, who handle relapses and emergencies. As a family member, you may have served as a caregiver yourself. Although this role can offer you satisfaction, it is often accompanied by frustration and sorrow as well.

Services

Like other people with mental illness, your relative may require a wide range of mental health, physical health, social, rehabilitative, vocational, and residential services. Unfortunately, these services are not always available—or always satisfactory when they are available. Researchers have documented many problems with the service delivery system, including the absence of treatment for large numbers of individuals with serious mental illness; the relative neglect of people with the most severe and persistent problems; inadequate funding for the full range of community-based services; and fragmentation of existing services. These problems may increase in our current era of managed care, which sometimes emphasizes the cost of services at the expense of their quality.

The consequences of these shortcomings are considerable for people with mental illness, whose lives may be marked by poverty, isolation, and abuse. On a given day approximately 3,500 inmates with mental illness are incarcerated in the Los Angeles County Jail—700 more than in the largest mental hospital in the nation. In fact, there are as many people with mental illness residing in our jails and prisons as in all of our hospitals. At least one-third of the homeless are estimated to have a mental illness—100,000 at any one time. Families pay the price for the absence of treatment in the criminal justice system and for people with mental illness who have joined the ranks of the homeless. As one sibling told us, "I see my brother in every disheveled and disoriented homeless person."

The following woman speaks for many family members who have confronted the limitations of the system:

> My sister was diagnosed with every term known to the psychiatric profession and given every related—and inappropriate—treatment. She is permanently handicapped with tardive dyskinesia. She was terribly abused in a state hospital where we had no rights to help her. Caring families get socked with most of the responsibility and blame but little legal or therapeutic support. We must change the system.

Another problem is the absence of services for family members, who often find the system insensitive to their anguish and unresponsive to their needs. One family member wrote: "I longed for someone to simply tell me what was happening to my father in terms that I could understand. This lack of knowledge about his illness contributed to my confusion and my feelings of helplessness as a child." In many studies, family members have reported unsatisfactory handling of crises and emergencies, insufficient communication and availability on the part of professionals, an absence of programs and services for families, and minimal involvement of families in treatment planning. Chances are your family has experienced many of these problems.

In addition to these failures, family members have also been adversely affected by earlier—and unsupported—theories that held "dysfunctional" or "pathogenic" families accountable for the mental illness. Thus, during a period of intense distress, family members may find that the system not only fails to address their expressed needs; they may also find that the system compounds their problems. Especially if your relative was diagnosed some years ago, your family may have shared the experience of the following sibling:

> I was part of a twins and siblings study. The viewpoint at that time was that the illness was caused by faulty parenting. I am angry at the doctors for blaming my parents, which hurt them as much as the tragedy of losing a daughter to mental illness. I recall no help for my pain. God knows it pretty much destroyed my parents.

Stigma

The final component of the objective burden is stigma, which often segregates and ostracizes people with mental illness. In fact, for many families stigma is the most debilitating handicap surrounding mental illness. Stigma has been described as a series of myths that serve to quarantine individuals with mental illness from the rest of society, branding any person seeking professional services with a mark of shame; isolating and punishing those in need of help; and legitimatizing the ridicule, humiliation, and dehumanization of people with mental illness.

There are many sources of stigma, including:

- our lack of understanding of mental illness and our fear of contagion and personal risk;

- our success-oriented society, which devalues people who cannot meet its exalted standards and defines dependence on others as moral failure;

- some professionals and other service providers, who hold an erroneous belief that mental illness is untreatable and irreversible; and

- the mass media, where mental illness is often portrayed in unrealistic, frightening, and disparaging ways.

In recent years there have been many encouraging developments, including the enactment in 1990 of the Americans with Disabilities Act, which offers protection from discrimination in the areas of employment, public transportation, and public accommodation. Nevertheless, stigmatization remains a pervasive problem for people with serious mental illness, for their families, and even for the professionals who work with this population. The adverse effects of stigma for family members may include lowered self-esteem and damaged family relationships, risk of self-stigmatization, and feelings of isolation and shame. As one family member told us, "The stigma has translated into an internalized feeling that something is wrong with me."

FAMILY RISKS

All family members are irrevocably changed by the presence of mental illness in their midst. The sinkhole of mental illness often depletes the emotional and financial resources of the family and creates fertile ground for conflict. Other time-limited disasters allow family members to replenish their depleted resources and to reestablish normal patterns of living. In contrast, mental illness is woven into the familial fabric on a continuing basis, with the potential for periodic emotional firestorms, recurrent crises, and indefinite expenditures of time, energy, and money.

The texture of family life is inevitably transformed by the onset of mental illness. Sometimes the family is reconstituted in constructive and adaptive ways; sometimes the family survives in anguish and disarray; and sometimes family bonds are broken beyond repair. As a family member, you may have experienced some of the following:

- denial of the mental illness by some members of your family, which can prevent them from coming to terms with the illness;

- family disruption and stress, which can diminish your family's energy and deplete their resources;

- maladaptive coping strategies used by your family members, such as substance abuse;

- family disintegration, if your family cannot withstand this assault on its integrity.

Denial

When family therapists use the phrase "the elephant in the living room," they are referring to significant problems that cannot be discussed openly. Family members may walk around the "elephant" and act as if it's not there, which may prevent painful feelings and conflicts from surfacing. But, of course, pretending there's no "elephant" also keeps family members from dealing with it—and from naming and taming.

There are many reasons why families treat mental illness as forbidden territory. Perhaps your family was poorly informed about the illness, thinking the symptoms were merely due to a difficult stage or life problem. At the onset of mental illness, there is often confusion about the diagnosis, the most appropriate treatment, and the expected outcome. In response to this confusion—and their own anguish—family members may deny the reality of the mental illness or minimize its seriousness. With knowledge and time, most families do adapt to the illness, although individual members may vary in their coping strategies, pacing, and ultimate degree of acceptance.

Sometimes family members internalize the corrosive stigma that pervades the larger society and retreat from their anguish behind a facade of conventionality, fearful that the "family secret" of mental illness will be revealed. This suppression keeps families from coping effectively. In the words of one family member, "If our family had only accepted that Mom was sick early on, then we could have dealt with the problem and had compassion for her instead of hostility. But the denial hamstrung us, caused us to fly apart."

Reflecting the larger society, your family may have accepted the belief that mental illness is something shameful to be avoided at all costs. Or perhaps the absence of communication reflected a more general tendency:

> Our family was never one to communicate, which didn't help my brother. Talk to each other about your feelings, even if it hurts. Be there for each other. Don't forget the siblings are also in pain. There is a life to be lived, even if the family is affected by this disease.

If your family was unable to deal with the mental illness in an open and constructive manner, their efforts undoubtedly added to your confusion and anguish. The following family member talks about this particular pattern:

> My mother devoted much of her life to trying to make my father appear "normal" to the outside world. Happiness was the only emotion that was acceptable for me to show in my family. I couldn't be sad. I was not allowed to get angry. To protect myself, I played the part of a good little girl. I was almost forty years old when I realized that I was still playing the same role!

Disruption and Stress

Most families do survive the catastrophic event of mental illness, but few do so without experiencing some family disruption and stress. In the words of one woman, " This terrible illness colors everything. A family cannot escape." Specific problems may include household disarray, financial difficulties, employment problems, strained marital and family relationships, impaired physical and mental health, and diminished social life. Like most families, your family has probably experienced some of these problems, at least occasionally. Some families confront many of them on a long-term basis, with little opportunity for respite. Under these circumstances, exhaustion and burnout are almost inevitable.

During crises, families often focus narrowly on managing the situation. When the crisis has passed, however, effective families return to a more balanced system designed to meet the essential needs of all members of the family. Unfortunately, some families remain frozen in a crisis mode or consumed by the illness, which prevents them from meeting the needs of well family members. One family member talked about her mother's two-year hospitalization, noting that it tore her family apart and placed her in an unwelcome role: "I had to be the little mother, since I was the oldest girl."

Although this pattern of long-term institutionalization is now relatively rare, many families face stressful periods. For example, people with mental illness are especially vulnerable to the overstimulation of holidays, which may trigger symptomatic behavior. The following woman describes one Christmas from her family's past. At the time, her brother resided in a state hospital, and her family decided to bring him home for the holiday. His refusal to take his medication precipitated the following episode:

His eyes were frightening, burning with a strange intensity. He continued the verbal abuse and then stood up, towering over me, and knocked me against the wall. I was on the phone to the police seconds later, terrified he was going to follow me into the room and hit me again. Finally the officers got him into the car, and he was taken to the local emergency room.

Maladaptive Coping Strategies

As families move through their life cycle, they cope with many expected and unexpected events. There is considerable variability in coping effectiveness among families and even across situations. Still, there are certain hallmarks of functional family coping, including the absence of physical violence and substance abuse. The problems of this multigenerational family member were exacerbated by the alcohol abuse of her well parent:

> My sister's illness became obvious as she reached puberty. She became withdrawn, socially inept, then began hearing voices. By the time I was in high school, my father suffered a "nervous breakdown" and began having wild mood swings. Mother was exhausted and had started drinking. I grew up suddenly, helping to run the household.

Family Disintegration

Mental illness can assault individuals and families with a vengeance, leaving behind a residue of damaged lives and ruptured relationships. Sometimes this assault results in partial or complete disintegration of the family, which can occur in several ways. For example, your relative may be lost to institutional care, to suicide, or to homelessness. Well family members may abandon the family in their effort to ensure their own preservation. Or children may be placed in foster care when their needs can no longer be met by their beleaguered family.

If you have experienced the mental illness of one parent and the withdrawal of your other parent, you can relate to the intense feelings of abandonment experienced by this multigenerational family member:

My mother was hospitalized when I was around seven or eight. There were awful fights, and eventually my father left when I was eleven. When my father left, we were just totally abandoned. There were five of us. My mother would go into rages and yell and scream. I didn't know anything about mental illness. We would just run and hide.

FAMILY RESILIENCE

Coping with the mental illness of a beloved relative presents a formidable challenge to *all* families. Yet families have their own powers of recuperation and renewal, often surviving their crises and meeting their challenges. Along with the family burden and risks that accompany a diagnosis of mental illness, your family also has the potential for a resilient response to a catastrophic event, which is characterized by:

- emergence of family strengths under challenging circumstances;

- persistence of family bonds;

- family pride over your accomplishments and those of your relative; and

- growth of your family as a unit and of your individual family members.

As you'll see, family resilience is a real part of the family experience of mental illness.

Family Strengths

Confronted with the mental illness of a member, all families struggle to adapt to this unanticipated event. Many families do manage to prevail over this family tragedy, to maintain the integrity of their family system, and to support their members. The following woman grew up with a brother who had schizophrenia, which was merely one event in a strong and effective family:

My husband once asked me how it was possible that I evolved unscathed from my upbringing with a mentally ill brother. It never occurred to me that as a family we should have fallen apart. To me my brother's illness was just a fact, like Daddy went to work on Monday mornings. It was okay for him to be that way, and it was okay for us to be happy. It was simple— you love your family, you care for each individual, you respect each other. It always felt solid, it felt right.

Family Bonds

As family members join forces to cope with the mental illness and its consequences, they may find their concerted action has reinforced the bonds that link them through time and space. Describing her family's commitment to each other, one woman wrote: "We have a strong feeling of family closeness. We never stopped trying and never stopped caring."

Family Pride

As family members learn to cope effectively with the mental illness in their midst, they may experience a sense of pride and satisfaction in their own accomplishments and those of their relative. The following woman has a brother with manic depression. Her family has served as a cornerstone of his support system, facilitating his recovery:

> We are proud of his progress. He lived at home, and we offered him a comfort zone that kept him out of the hospital. I always tried to be stable, calm, and understanding. I helped my brother maintain his reality contact. He has had the support of his family. I never forget that it could have been me.

Family Growth

Through time, family members acquire essential information about mental illness and community resources, develop effective coping skills, and often change in constructive ways. Here is one man's description of his family:

It was a strong family before my mother's illness. It's gotten much stronger since. We enjoy being around each other. We have discussed my mother's illness with each other and with her therapist. Just because there is mental illness in a family doesn't mean the family has to stop growing as a unit or that the person cannot lead a constructive life.

Looking Beyond the Mental Illness

All families share in the family burden, family risks, and family resilience that accompany the mental illness of a close relative. But the illness is only one event in your larger family context. Your family's experience of mental illness is also defined by their particular strengths and resources. In addition to the characteristics of effective families discussed earlier, important resources include:

- good mental and physical health among your family members;

- adequate financial and educational resources;

- a strong support system, both inside and outside your family; and

- spiritual resources that give meaning and coherence to life.

Likewise, other problems in your family are likely to magnify your family's burden and undermine their coping effectiveness. These include:

- separation, divorce, or other losses;

- chronic medical problems or disabilities;

- substance abuse;

- child abuse or domestic violence;

- unemployment or job-related problems; and

- poverty.

If your family faced any of these additional problems, you are well aware of their potential damage. One family member wrote about suffering "the dual taboos of mental illness and divorce" when her parents divorced as a result of her father's illness. Another recalls the fear for her own safety that propelled her from her home:

> I left home at thirteen. I would just run away. When my schizophrenic brother would strike out, I was afraid for my safety. I tried numerous times to get into foster-care or group homes. I finally got out by getting pregnant and married. They couldn't send me back then. After I left, my brother sexually abused my younger sister.

INDIVIDUAL FAMILY MEMBERS

So far we've focused on the family experience of mental illness—the burden, risks, and resilience shared by all members of your family. But each member of your family also has unique experiences, needs, and concerns. In turn, all of their experiences have affected you. Your family is like a mobile—a sculpture of wire and colored shapes that can be set in motion by movement in one part, which in turn affects the whole construction. Changes in individuals affect the family system in much the same way.

Your family mobile changes through time, reflecting the metamorphosis of individual shapes, the fluctuations in family roles and relationships, and the gusts that blow from inside and outside your family. But always these individual shapes are joined to others in the family mobile— by a complex web of shared history, sorrows, and triumphs.

Your Relative with Mental Illness

In this chapter we've emphasized the impact of mental illness on your family. But we haven't yet talked about mental illness from the perspective of your relative—the person most affected by the illness. We recently conducted a survey of people with mental illness, asking them to tell us about their experience with the illness. They told us about their many losses—of relationships, educational opportunities, jobs, and money, as well as of hopes, dreams, and expectations:

I became unable to continue my senior year in college. I am also unable to work because I need the daily support of partial hospitalization. I've lost all of my friends except one because of the stigma associated with mental illness.

They talked about changes in their self-concept as a result of the mental illness. One person wrote: "I have low self-esteem, feel alone and very lonely." But another was more hopeful:

At first I hit rock bottom in almost every area in my life and began to vegetate. But with good therapy, good doctors, help from within, and God's grace, I am at a wonderful point in life now. I have regained my self-respect.

They also commented on family relationships, again noting the potential for both negative changes, such as stress and disruption, and for positive changes, such as closer family ties. In addition, many of our participants described a process of adaptation and recovery:

The illness itself has not had any good effects, but the process of getting healthier has, especially on my spirituality, my self-image, and my character and personal qualities. Now I have a greater sense of serenity, self-liking, wonder at the world, and caring for myself and others.

Our participants shared the coping resources and strategies that had helped them in their recovery process. One wrote: "Believe in yourself. Have courage, be determined not to give up." Others emphasized the value of professional treatment: "Treatment works—seek professional help. Learn everything you can about your illness, medication, and treatment." And still others emphasized the value of social support: "If people don't understand your illness, don't worry about it. Just go on. Get in a support group and make friends with people with similar problems."

Parents

When a child of any age develops mental illness, parents generally experience a wide range of intense losses, both real and symbolic. They may undergo a grieving process over the loss of the well child for whom there was so much potential. In addition, parents frequently become primary caregivers, which may become the central event of their lives. Especially at the onset of the illness, they may experience significant marital distress, as they struggle to deal with the mental health system and to understand the meaning of mental illness for their child, for their family, and for themselves.

Mothers carry a special burden when a child has a mental illness. They are likely to bear primary responsibility for caregiving, sometimes for a lifetime; to experience identity problems in a world where female identity remains precariously dependent on successful offspring; and to be chastised by earlier professional theories that held them accountable for the mental illness. In the words of one mother, "The problems with my daughter were like a black hole inside of me into which everything else had been drawn."

Fathers also experience a heavy burden. Traditional fathers are likely to have difficulty fulfilling their role as protector and resolving their powerful emotional burden. Contemporary fathers, who are more involved in the nurturing of their children, also share more fully in the emotional and caregiving burden that accompanies a child's mental illness.

If you are a sibling, the experiences of your parents alter your family life and your relationships with each of them. If your mother becomes consumed with the mental illness of your brother or sister, you may miss her emotional availability and nurturing. Similarly, if your father disengages from the painful family situation, you may lose a precious companion and role model. As one family member has expressed it, "You lose not only your sibling but also your parents as they become overwhelmed and embroiled."

At the same time, many parents do manage to cope with the mental illness of their child, to sustain their family, and to achieve a balance that meets the needs of all family members. This woman was only seven years old when her older sister developed schizophrenia. Yet her family was able to meet the needs of their other children, and she felt loved and cherished as she was growing up:

> Amazingly, despite the presence of this horrible illness in our
> lives, my childhood was, in many ways, a normal one. I took
> piano lessons, went to camp. My parents took us on vacations

and out to dinner. They attended all of the important milestones in my childhood. I never doubted their love for me.

Spouses

In addition to the common family burden, spouses often experience a range of emotional, social, and financial losses similar to those that accompany the death of a husband or wife. Spouses are faced with increased responsibility for parenting and other aspects of family life, and often struggle to balance their own needs with those of other family members. They may experience substantial conflict and guilt if they consider separation or divorce:

> I decided the only way out was to get a divorce. It wasn't easy. I still had feelings for my husband, but I couldn't live with him. He said that I was the one who was at fault with this divorce because we married "for better, for worse, in sickness and health." He says I'm the one who didn't live up to our marriage vows.

If your ill relative is your mother or father, you are also deeply affected by the response of your well parent. If that parent is overwhelmed and aggrieved by the mental illness, or if your parents divorce as a result of the illness, your own losses will be compounded. Both parents may be less available to meet your needs, one parent because of the illness and the other because of the altered family situation. Under these circumstances, you may feel you have lost both parents; in some ways, you have. As one adult offspring wrote, "My dad also abandoned us, in the emotional sense, becoming so confused and devastated that he was oblivious to our feelings and unable to help us deal with them."

Still, we have heard from family members whose parents have managed to build a strong and enduring marriage in spite of the mental illness. One woman described the marriage of her parents as follows: "At heart, my mother was a lovely, gentle person. My father loved her for fifty-seven years."

Siblings

If you are a sibling, clearly you have a special vulnerability. Siblings are usually partners in our longest relationship. Often, they know us like no one else and strongly influence our personality and relationships throughout our lives. When one sibling develops a mental illness, the losses are enormous for their brothers and sisters.

As a sibling, you may have experienced dual losses, both of your brother or sister and of your parents, who may be consumed in their own grief. You may also be at risk for unresolved grief if your own losses are not acknowledged, for a "replacement child syndrome" if you attempt to compensate your anguished parents for the mental illness of your sibling, and for alienation from the "normal" world of your peers.

Even when one has a mental illness, sibling pairs share in the gratifications and risks that accompany all of our intimate relationships. Here are the comments of two women who have brothers with mental illness. They bear witness to both poles of the sibling bond:

> My brother was diagnosed as paranoid schizophrenic. His pain has taken its toll on our family. It is a terrible feeling to watch someone that you love go through such torment. I feel so helpless and filled with such sorrow for him. When I look into his eyes (and sometimes I can't even do that), I know he'll never be the same.

> It's valuable for my brother to have siblings. We're a major part of his social life and he enjoys our visits. He's made puzzles and crafts for my daughter. She visits him, and he shows her his inventions and hobbies. He's fun, interesting, and entertaining—he makes me smile. I love his wit.

In reality, over the course of your life you are likely to experience both poles of this relationship.

In addition, you are likely to be affected by the response of your well siblings, who carry their own burden. If they remain consumed by their grief or attempt to survive by disengaging from the family, you may also experience the loss of their support, advice, companionship, and protection. Even under difficult circumstances, however, our brothers and sisters can create a sibling support system that functions as a loving safety net, balancing the family losses and sustaining us throughout our lives.

Offspring

If you have a parent with mental illness, you are well aware of the terrible toll paid by offspring. Parents are at the center of our earliest relationship, essential for our physical and psychological survival. Throughout our lives, they serve as our teachers, role models, and objects of identification. When a parent has mental illness, the losses for their offspring may be enormous, including the loss of love, comfort, guidance, and validation.

As someone who was exposed to psychotic thinking early in life, you may have become enveloped in the disturbed thoughts and feelings of your parent. One family member told us it was years before she could sort out what was real about her neighbors and what reflected her mother's paranoid views. Perhaps your own needs were neglected as your parent struggled for survival. Or you may have shouldered adult responsibilities or aspired to be a perfect child to spare your family additional grief—too heavy a burden for any young family member.

Yet not all parents with mental illness are ineffective parents, nor are all of their offspring unable to cope. In fact, parents and offspring are both diverse groups who need to be described in terms of their strengths as well as their limitations. This diversity is reflected in the accounts of the following family members. Both grew up with the mental illness of a beloved parent:

> I recall clearly the feelings of guilt, fear, anger, grief, and mistrust. I now understand how they affected my life. Why did my father's mental illness affect me so? Because mental illness becomes a family illness, regardless of who carries its symptoms. It reaches out and scars the life of each family member. No one walks away unaffected.

> I feel that being a concerned family member has helped me become a better person in many ways. I learned to become self-sufficient at an early age. I am gratified that I helped my mother. I am a person who enjoys being alive despite having had the trauma of an adolescence with a severely mentally ill parent.

As with most family members, over time you have probably experienced both ends of this spectrum, sharing in the emotional burden of the first family member and in the resilience of the second.

Multigenerational Family Members

Multigenerational family members are those who have both a sibling and a parent with mental illness. If you have more than one relative with mental illness, you may feel you have a certain grim heritage. As other families are influenced by a history of politics or poetry, yours is defined by a history of mental illness.

Multigenerational family members share in the experiences of both siblings and offspring—in many respects a dual grieving process and a double legacy. As someone who experienced the mental illness of his mother and three siblings, Rex speaks about the distinctive impact of mental illness on each bond:

> Since I did not know my mother prior to her illness, the impact on me has been less of a loss and more of a void. I suspect there are reservoirs of sadness for me and for my mother that are associated with this emptiness. Sibling effects are immediate, whereas the deeper effects of a parent may take longer to surface. The "hole in the soul" as a result of my mother's disorder has been less tangible, yet more profound.

Other Relatives

When we think of family members, we often forget about grandparents, aunts, uncles, and cousins. Yet these family members too may be profoundly affected by the mental illness in their extended family. They may share in the subjective and objective burden shouldered by the rest of the family. Extended family members can also offer life-enhancing love and support, as in the case of the following sibling:

> My mother's aunt and uncle, who were in essence our grandparents, were an enormous help to my mother, my sister, and me. For my entire childhood they lived right down the street from us and were a shelter when needed.

The Family Mobile

Over a lifetime you and your family members will each dance to your own tempo and cadence. Alternately, each of you will give and receive support, seek and avoid closeness, pursue your personal and family goals, and perhaps assume or avoid caregiving responsibilities for your relative. The mental illness can bring a special intensity to these normal cycles of family cohesion and disengagement, intensifying the inevitable conflicts in family relationships. But with time, your family may be able to create a mobile that joins the individual pieces with love and compassion into a resplendent whole:

> I started to understand how difficult it must have been for my family and how they did the best they could. I was able to forgive them and forgive myself for all the anger I had for them. My mother and I can now discuss what has happened and empathize with each other.

MILEPOSTS

In completing the family leg of your journey of hope and healing, you've reached the following mileposts:

- increased knowledge of the disruptive effects of mental illness on your family system;

- better understanding of your family burden, risks, and resilience; and

- greater awareness of the impact of mental illness on your individual family members.

During the next leg, you'll see how the family experience affected your own life.

Chapter 3

RECLAIMING YOUR
CHILDHOOD

❧

*I became the perfect child to spare my parents more grief. I was
forced to become responsible. In many ways it forced me to accomplish things in my life I might not have otherwise done. But I have
spent my life trying to run away from this problem. Feeling guilty
and helpless, the unending sorrow for not being able to help. I have
not felt entitled to be happy most of my adult life.*

R ECALLING HER EARLY encounter with her brother's mental
illness, this family member remembers feeling torn between a
desire to rescue her brother and fear that her own life would be
sacrificed in the process. For two decades she remained in a state of perpetual conflict.

As someone who grew up with mental illness in your family, you
probably shared some of her feelings. You may have tried to mold yourself into a perfect child, assuming adult responsibilities that weighed
heavily on your young shoulders. Perhaps you invested strongly in
achievements outside your family, partly to compensate your aggrieved
family, partly to rebuild your sagging self-esteem, and partly to escape
from your family situation. Yet because this tragic family event was
woven into the texture of your identity, you carried it with you—into the
world outside your family and into your adulthood.

Whatever the specific effects of your relative's mental illness, your developmental path was transformed from the moment the illness erupted in your family. As one woman expressed it, "I have been burned to my very core." In the last chapter we explored the impact of mental illness on your family as a whole and on your individual family members. In the second leg of your journey, we'll look more closely at the personal meaning of your family experience—what we've called the SaC (Sibling and Child) Syndrome.

Chances are you have been largely unaware of the pervasive impact of the mental illness on your life. There are many reasons for this lack of awareness, including the conspiracy of silence that frequently prevents families from talking openly about the illness and the social stigma that so often alienates and isolates them. In addition, especially if you were very young at the time of your initial encounter with mental illness, you may have partially cut off painful memories, images, or feelings (the dissociation we discussed earlier), or tried to shut down your emotional life (psychic numbing).

Now, as you name and tame your experiences, a kaleidoscope of fragments—the earlier issues you avoided—may resurface with intensity. Although this emotional flooding may temporarily increase your distress, you have an opportunity to confront and reclaim your early years.

LANDMARKS

This leg of your journey includes three important landmarks. First, you'll find out about the special vulnerability you share with other young family members.

Second, you'll learn about the ways in which mental illness affected your life inside and outside your family circle, and about the shared concerns and risks of siblings and offspring.

Finally, you'll discover your potential for a resilient response to your difficult family circumstances.

Each of these topics will give you a chance to understand and master your past, probably for the first time in your life.

VULNERABILITY OF YOUNG FAMILY MEMBERS

As someone who grew up with mental illness in your family, you have a special vulnerability. In fact, our research highlights the importance of your age at the onset of your relative's illness. In essence, the younger you were at the onset, the greater the potential impact on your life. There are two reasons for your greater vulnerability as a young child.

The first is the limited capacity of children to deal with disruptive or traumatic events. Compared with adolescents or adults, children have fewer coping skills and strategies for dealing with a threatening event, and are more easily overwhelmed. For example, in light of their immaturity, they have less ability to understand the complexity of mental illness and to verbalize their painful feelings. In addition, children are more dependent on the other people in their lives, a precarious position when a caregiver suffers from mental illness. And because young family members are exposed to the mental illness while their personality is still developing, this disruptive event is woven into their emerging sense of self—becoming part of them rather than something that happens to them.

The second reason is the nature of human development, which is often viewed in terms of a series of stages, each with its accompanying tasks. As we complete the tasks of one stage, we lay the foundation for the next stage. Any disruptive event, such as mental illness, may prevent us from accomplishing our developmental tasks, leaving us "stuck" in a particular stage and with a residue of unfinished business for the future. In your own case, the unfinished business consists of any tasks that were interrupted, postponed, or canceled by the presence of the mental illness in your family.

Here are the words of a multigenerational family member whose unfinished business profoundly affected her adult years:

> I am just learning, at age forty-nine, that I can be me. I have only just begun to identify what I want and who I really am. I adapted my behavior at home totally in the interest of keeping the equilibrium in the family. I felt responsible for making everyone happy. I took on emotions of others as something I had to fix. I developed a pattern of putting others before myself, lost my identity in relationships.

The timing of the mental illness in your life is especially important. We'll chart some of the important tasks at each stage of development, which will offer an opportunity for you to think about your early experience with mental illness and the ways in which your developmental tasks may have been affected.

Early Childhood

During the first five years of life, infants and preschoolers face a number of important developmental tasks. Because of their prolonged dependency, they are reliant on their human and physical environment. A deficient or dangerous environment places their very survival at risk. Tasks of the first two years reflect the significance of our early relationships, including:

- attachment, as infants bond with their earliest caregivers and build a foundation for future relationships; and

- the establishment of basic trust, which requires a relatively secure and nurturing environment.

From ages three to five, preschoolers acquire many of the competencies that will allow them to function effectively in the world outside their family. The tasks of this period center on:

- socialization, as children acquire the knowledge, skills, values, and behaviors that will enable them to participate in their society; and

- self-concept, including a sense of being a valuable and competent person.

If you were exposed to mental illness in your first five years of life, each of these tasks may have been affected. For instance, your sense of basic trust and security may have been shaken by a parent whose own energy was consumed by the illness, whose reality contact was sometimes impaired, or whose false beliefs and distorted perceptions were presented as real. Similarly, the mental illness may have drained family energy needed to help you acquire essential knowledge about your world and develop a healthy self-concept.

The following family member talks about her struggle to establish a secure sense of self in the wake of her mother's schizophrenia:

> Most of my adult life has been spent "constructing me." My self-concept makes me work the hardest. On a very deep level, I know that my own survival depends on not giving in to my terrible feelings of low self-worth.

Middle Childhood

As children shift from their home to the larger social context in middle childhood, they learn new academic and interpersonal skills. Their developmental tasks focus on:

- academic adjustment, as children acquire the basic building blocks that allow them to succeed in our society; and

- peer relationships, as they establish a social network outside their family.

During middle childhood, children develop new interests in school and in peer relationships. But if you lacked a secure foundation as your world expanded, you may have felt unprepared for the world outside your family and remained preoccupied with problems at home. For example, one family member remembers sitting in class and being unable to concentrate, "all of my energy directed toward what was happening at home and what was going to become of our family."

Adolescence

Adolescents who are preparing for an independent and productive adulthood confront a new set of issues. Some of the most important include:

- forging a sense of personal identity that can serve as an internal compass in a world in flux;

- coming to terms with emerging sexuality in a world of changing sex roles, values, standards, and behaviors;

- charting a tentative career path that can guide educational and vocational plans and goals; and

- achieving separation and departing for an uncertain future.

If you were dealing with mental illness as a teenager, accomplishment of all of these tasks may have been undermined. You may have worried about developing mental illness yourself as you formed a stable identity. Perhaps you found that your feelings of loss and isolation interfered with your ability to form close relationships or to begin dating. Possibly your family responsibilities deterred you from making educational and career plans or from separating from a family that had come to depend on you.

Rex talks about some of his own difficulties as a teenager, when his mother's paranoid thinking curtailed his interest in dating:

> Our mother warned us to guard against "the hussies who are looking to get pregnant and ruin your future." I absorbed some of the ominous, confused, free-floating sexual and relationship fears of my mother. One false move and I would plunge into a cauldron of human passions.

Take a minute to consider the impact of mental illness on your own developmental tasks. If you were exposed to mental illness from your earliest years, virtually all of your tasks may have been affected, leaving you with a legacy of unfinished business that has colored your entire life. Likewise, if you were in elementary, junior high, or high school at the time of the onset, you may have failed to complete the tasks associated with those periods.

Throughout your childhood and adolescence, your risks fell into four general areas: developmental risks, family roles and relationships, academic life, and peer relationships.

DEVELOPMENTAL RISKS

The mental illness of a family member is an unexpected event that disrupts the usual sense of continuity and rhythm in the life cycle, with a profound impact on young family members. As a sibling or offspring of someone with mental illness, you faced a number of developmental risks:

- that your own needs might be neglected;
- that your own development might be hindered;
- that you might have to grow up too quickly; and
- that you might have difficulty separating from your family.

Neglect of Your Needs

In our research, family members who were exposed to mental illness during their first decade of life sometimes said that their family's struggle with the illness resulted in neglect of their own needs. In fact, 79 percent of our survey participants felt their needs had been neglected as they were growing up; 61 percent reported a sense of abandonment. As one multigenerational family member declared, "My needs were not met when I was growing up."

Hindered Personal Development

In order to proceed in their development, young family members need to grow up as valued members of the family, to be supported and educated by the adults in their family, and to be encouraged to pursue their interests. Sometimes the mental illness consumes so much of the family's energy that little is left for the well children. As a multigenerational family member, Rex talks about the impact of his family situation on his early years:

> Since birth, I had been an emotional orphan, but I didn't know it. At some level, my parents could not relate to me, to each other, or to themselves. Like weeds along a roadside, my siblings and I grew up in random fashion, to a large degree

untended and unminded. Navigating a path into adulthood would be difficult.

When you were growing up, you may have been confused by your relative's symptoms and even drawn into the psychotic system, as this family member was: "My mother has been sick practically my whole life. It is hard for me to decipher which of my experiences are 'normal' and which are not." Or perhaps you identified with an adored parent or older sibling, modeling inappropriate patterns of behavior. The following woman was pulled into her mother's psychotic world:

> When Mom first became ill, I remember consciously deciding to join in with her wild adventures, thinking she would like me more, love me more, if I did. Rather than ever let on that I thought her new life was crazy or how hurt I felt from her abandonment and personality change, I tried to embrace it, or at least accept it.

Similarly, this sibling continued to identify with a brother who no longer served as a constructive role model. Even after the onset of his brother's mental illness, he looked up to and imitated his brother:

> When he went crazy, I took drugs to be like him. I even moved into his bedroom when he was hospitalized. I was feeling the pain of my brother and was more depressed—a lingering sadness, pain in my heart. I wanted to save him, to sacrifice myself to help him, to get our separated family back together.

Growing Up Too Quickly

In some cases, family members may shoulder heavy family responsibilities before they have finished being children, sacrificing their own childhood in their effort to meet the needs of their family. More than two-thirds of our participants felt they had grown up too quickly. As a family member, you may have shared in this woman's sense of a lost childhood:

I lost out in my childhood. Most of my memories include a sickly older sister who got all the attention by having repeated crises. So I was left to my own devices a lot. I have always had to be responsible.

Separation Problems

As they mature, children must separate from their families, first leaving their secure home base for school and later departing for an independent adulthood. The mental illness in your family may have undermined your separation process in several ways, as it did for 51 percent of our participants. For example, if your needs were not met by your overwhelmed family, you may have failed to develop the resources necessary for coping effectively with the adult world.

Or possibly you found it difficult to separate from a family that had come to depend on you, experiencing significant guilt when you did leave home. One woman wrote about her own separation problems: "I had a hard time moving away. I felt guilty all the time. It was difficult to keep my mind on my studies in college."

FAMILY ROLES AND RELATIONSHIPS

Even the most stable family is likely to be unsettled by the many changes that have beset families in recent years. For families of people with mental illness, there are far greater risks of altered roles and relationships as a result of the illness. As a young family member, you may have experienced some of the following:

- distorted family roles and relationships in response to the disruptive force of mental illness;

- parentification, if you assumed a parental role as a child;

- a replacement child syndrome, if you sought to compensate your parents for the mental illness of your brother or sister;

- a survivor's syndrome, if you experienced guilt for having been spared mental illness yourself.

Distorted Roles and Relationships

Mental illness sometimes prevents family members from fulfilling their expected functions. The mental illness of your mother or father may have kept your parents from meeting their responsibilities inside or outside your family. Likewise, the mental illness of your brother or sister may have consumed so much parental energy that little remained for meeting your needs. In the aftermath of this catastrophic event, all of your family roles may have been shuffled and all of your relationships transformed. As a result of her mother's mental illness, for example, this woman developed an unhealthy relationship with her father that undermined her later relationships with men:

> As the eldest daughter I had a unique relationship with my father. I became his confidant and fellow decision maker in the family. This relationship was comforting, and I clung to it emotionally. Little did I realize how unhealthy it was, until as an adult I have had great difficulty in my relationships with men as a result.

Parentification

Parentification occurs when young family members assume parental roles before they have finished being children themselves. As a family member, you may have tried to lighten your family's burden by assuming adult responsibilities. Or perhaps you were propelled into a premature maturity by other members of your family. This woman talks about her assumption of a parental role after the onset of her mother's mental illness:

> There were seven of us in the home, and I had to take my mother's role. I wasn't allowed to be a child—my brothers and sisters could be children. My mother was never there for me. I never looked up to her as a mother. I felt burdened and resented it.

Replacement Child Syndrome

Children who have experienced the death of a sibling may seek to become perfect children to compensate their aggrieved parents or try to accommodate parents who seek a substitute for their stricken child. The "replacement child syndrome" may also occur among children who have experienced the serious mental illness of a brother or sister. This sibling describes the role reversal that resulted from her brother's schizophrenia:

> The change in my status within my family has been difficult. After all, my brother was the genius with enormous potential. Now, with his illness, by default I am the star in the family. My parents, their hopes miserably shattered by my brother, now rise and fall with me through my every peak and valley. That is the load I carry now, and I hate it.

Survivor's Syndrome

As someone who has a close relative with mental illness, you may have experienced a "survivor's syndrome" that subjected you to feelings of guilt for having been spared, preventing you from deriving pleasure from your own life. This family member, who has two siblings with mental illness, talks about his survivor's guilt:

> The guilt that you feel can be debilitating. A lot of times you don't want to have success. You cover up your success because the ill family member is missing so many good things in life. And you feel bad about getting those yourself. If you have a girlfriend or fiancée, you want to play that down.

Academic Life

Adult siblings and offspring often observe that their experience with mental illness has affected their academic life. One family member wrote: "I questioned my own mental health. I slowly lost interest in my studies, and my grades dropped." As a young family member, your schoolwork may have seemed trivial compared with the struggle for survival occurring at home. Or perhaps you were fearful that the disruption at home would spill over into the school setting.

Some of the possible effects of mental illness on your academic life include:

- poor school performance resulting from the disruption at home;

- superachievement at school, which may have diverted you from coming to terms with the mental illness;

- an adverse impact on your extracurricular activities; and

- altered educational and career plans in response to the needs of your family.

Poor School Performance

Along with many other young family members, you may have had difficulty performing in school. Poor school performance may have further eroded your low self-esteem. Possibly your feelings of underachievement were reinforced by teachers or guidance counselors who noted your uneven performance but were unaware of the source. This woman recalls her early fear that her father's mental illness would disrupt her life at school:

> Very much of my young life was affected. I had trouble concentrating in school, was afraid Dad would appear at the school grounds when he was sick. I could not bring any school friends home for fear that they would not understand. Mom was busy working full time to make ends meet. Not much time was spent helping me get prepared for school.

Superachievement

Young family members may escape from their feelings of hopelessness and helplessness by immersing themselves in activities outside their home. Often this is a constructive reallocation of energy that offers opportunities for growth and satisfaction. However, an immersion in outside activities may be counterproductive if it prevents you from confronting this pivotal event in your life or leaves you unduly dependent on external validation:

> I became an overachiever at school and withdrew emotionally from my family. I grew increasingly dependent on scholastic and then business achievements at the expense of a rich personal life. I have problems in establishing and maintaining intimate relationships. Through the help of therapy, I am now learning how much of it has to do with my family.

Extracurricular Activities

Extracurricular activities offer many opportunities for children and adolescents to enhance their skills and self-esteem, to expand activities and relationships outside their family, to obtain reinforcement for normal developmental experiences and goals, and to identify with constructive role models. Unfortunately, as a young family member you may have found yourself foreclosed from these potential benefits because of your feelings of social alienation and isolation. The following family member describes a cloistered life that excluded peer relationships and extracurricular activities:

> I started working part time at age 14, and that kept me so busy that I didn't have time to think about how isolated I was from other people my age. I felt unattractive and unlovable in high school and didn't date. I never felt safe enough to rebel. I continued throughout my adolescence to be a "good girl."

Altered Educational and Career Plans

The continuing demands of the mental illness may have depleted your family's emotional and financial resources, with negative consequences for your educational and career plans. Perhaps your parents offered you little encouragement as you charted your vocational course. Or possibly you had difficulty focusing on your own future when your family was in such disarray. The next woman reflects on the consequences of her sister's schizophrenia for her own life:

The pain and grief made it impossible for me to enjoy the "best years" of my life. This is a time when you are trying to determine your career and future, but you are too busy trying to understand mental illness. Accepting that my sister will never live a normal life, that we will never enjoy a normal sister-to-sister relationship, that I will need to be more responsible for her care.

For other family members, educational success can offer an opportunity to enhance self-esteem and to identify with constructive role models. You may have shared the satisfaction of this woman in academic accomplishments:

Education has always been an anchor for me. College enabled me to have a new identity, where I could not be constantly reminded of my depressing family situation. School was the one thing my parents couldn't mess up with their excesses and unpredictable behavior. Something positive when the rest of my life was in shambles.

PEER RELATIONSHIPS

Early relationships within the family serve as a prototype for later relationships outside the family. When family relationships are adversely affected by the presence of mental illness, young family members may have unsatisfactory models for later peer relationships. These relationships may also be undermined by the sense of social estrangement that often accompanies the mental illness of a close relative. As a young family member, you may have experienced some of the following:

- problems in peer relationships resulting from the mental illness in your family;

- a sense of social deviance that leaves you a perpetual outsider;

- difficulty straddling the different worlds inside and outside your family; and

- absence of a secure home base due to the unpredictable and disruptive presence of mental illness.

Problems in Peer Relationships

As you were growing up, you may have felt estranged from your "normal" peers, tainted by the corrosive effects of stigma, and alienated from people who couldn't begin to understand your family situation. Perhaps you responded to your relative's illness in ways that adversely affected your other relationships. For example, this woman learned to distance herself from the symptoms of her father's mental illness, a pattern that generalized to her other relationships:

> I began to distance myself from those whom I loved, not just my mentally ill father. If I felt wronged by a friend or hurt by a sibling, I would pull away from them, never addressing the painful issue. I would ignore the hurt, pretending to be unaffected by it. Then I would try to stay emotionally distanced so that the chance to be hurt again could never even occur.

Sense of Social Deviance

The stigmatization that accompanies a diagnosis of serious mental illness often has devastating consequences for family members. Young family members may grow up with a sense of social deviance that pervades their lives and that leaves them feeling like outsiders in the world outside their family. One family member wrote: "Community members, relatives, and friends retreat from a situation they do not understand." As a sibling or offspring, you may have experienced lowered self-esteem, a tendency toward self-stigmatization, and feelings of isolation and shame. This sibling shares some of these feelings:

> I knew my sister was different. I was torn between loyalty to her and wanting to be accepted by my friends. The pain and sense of being different were already there. I felt unacceptable to my peers and restricted my friendships to a few people who accepted me and did not ask too many questions.

Straddling Two Worlds

As they are growing up, family members often have a sense of standing with one foot in the "abnormal" world of their family and one foot in the "normal" world of their peers. Struggling to straddle the two worlds inside and outside your family, you may have shared this woman's desperate quest to appear normal:

> I worked very hard at being normal away from home, because I knew that what awaited me when I got home was more bizarre than anyone would believe. I felt best when I was normally active—working on the yearbook, biking with my friends, going on school trips, having fun with my friends, doing well in school. Being considered normal was my greatest salvation. Inside I felt like a total freak.

Absence of a Secure Home Base

In a sometimes hostile world, families can offer a safe haven that nurtures and protects its members. When your family includes a member with mental illness, that sense of security may be undermined. Rex talks about his own family environment, conveying the vulnerability that young children may experience when exposed to parental mental illness:

> Often, we children would lie in bed feigning sleep, listening to the rising crescendo of voices. My parents said such horrible, destructive things to one another. There was always the danger that things would spin out of control. I had my own escape plan—which window to jump from, where to land, where to run, where to hide—all, just in case.

CONCERNS OF FAMILY MEMBERS

In probing the personal meaning of mental illness, you've seen that the illness is likely to affect all aspects of your life, including your feelings about yourself, as well as your relationships inside and outside your family. In our research with adult siblings and offspring, we explored some of the common concerns related to their family experience. The following were cited most frequently (the percentage refers to the number of respondents who experienced this concern):

Concerns of Adult Siblings and Offspring

- Concern about caregiving for their relative (94%)

- Family disruption (83%)

- Difficulty balancing personal and family needs (81%)

- Sense that their own needs had not been met (79%)

- Feelings of helplessness and hopelessness (75%)

- Poor self-esteem (75%)

- Guilt feelings (74%)

- Psychic numbing (70%)

- Problems trusting (69%)

- Problems with intimacy (69%)

- Sense of growing up too fast (67%)

- Personal depression (66%)

- Chronic sorrow (64%)

- Sense of unfulfilled potential (64%)

- Need to be perfect (63%)

- Grieving process (63%)

- Sense of abandonment (61%)

- Identity problems (59%)

- Fear of violence (57%)

- Social isolation (54%)

(continued on page 62)

- Fear of suicide (52%)

- Effect on personal choices (51%)

- Difficulty separating from their family (51%)

Undoubtedly, as a family member you share some of these concerns. Along with almost all of our participants, you may worry about your caregiving responsibilities in the present or in an uncertain future. For example, adult offspring often assume a central role in caregiving for parents who have mental illness, sometimes on a long-term basis:

> When I was eighteen, I became my mother's caretaker. My mother lived with me until she died. I married, had children, and took care of Mother throughout my whole life. That placed our family under severe emotional stress. Every stressful life experience precipitated a crisis in which Mother's hallucinations or delusions were exacerbated.

The pattern of caregiving is more variable among siblings, who are comparatively free to define their adult relationships and to choose their extent of involvement. Although the following woman is not involved in daily caregiving, she sometimes serves as a resource for her sister under crisis conditions:

> My sister often functions at a high level. She is single, has her own apartment, and works for a major company. Every year or two she has been hospitalized for mania. She thought her plane had a bomb on it, fled the plane, and eventually was arrested. I spent a week as her advocate—dealt with lawyers, doctors, magistrates, and mental health workers. This was the most intense and worst week of my life.

In addition to caregiving, you may experience the other concerns mentioned by our participants. You may have shared their sense of family disruption and their struggle to balance their own needs with those of their families. As a child perhaps you felt your needs were not met or you had been pressured to grow up too fast.

On a more personal level, you may have confronted their feelings of helplessness and hopelessness. Possibly you have suffered from low self-esteem, guilt, perfectionism, psychic numbing, or problems with trust and intimacy. And with so many family members, you may have experienced intense feelings of loss and grief, as well as an undercurrent of chronic sorrow that was woven into your life.

These concerns constitute a powerful legacy. In addition, as a family member, you carry a small but increased risk of developing mental illness yourself. In contrast to a 1 percent incidence of schizophrenia in the general population, for example, the lifetime risk of developing schizophrenia among siblings and offspring is around 10 percent. But we want to emphasize that you have about a 90 percent chance of *NOT* developing mental illness. Furthermore, because mental illness most often develops in late adolescence or early adulthood, if you are over thirty, your risk has decreased significantly.

In our experience, adult siblings and offspring are very likely to overestimate their personal risk. For instance, a sibling at one of our workshops expressed concern about developing schizophrenia. When asked to estimate his risk, he responded 80 percent—eight times higher than his actual risk! Even people with no mental illness in their families have a propensity to worry about their mental health. Undoubtedly, this propensity is stronger among family members. Thus, it is essential for you to keep in mind that your personal risk is relatively low and to guard against becoming overly anxious.

PERSONAL RESILIENCE

So far we've focused on the risks and concerns you share with other family members. But that's only part of the picture. As a close relative of someone with mental illness, you also have the capacity for a resilient response to this family tragedy. Resilience is the ability to rebound from early adversity and to prevail over the circumstances of your life.

Resilient individuals may have experienced considerable suffering in their childhood. But often with much difficulty and over a period of many years, they have emerged as better and stronger people. They have the courage to face their past and have accepted their earlier losses without bitterness or anger, viewing their family with understanding, compassion, and generosity. They have achieved insight into the SaC Syndrome and its meaning for their lives, applying the lessons of the past to live better in the present, and assuming ownership of their lives and responsibility for their actions.

Resilient individuals view the world and themselves in positive but realistic terms. They look for and acknowledge the strengths in themselves and others, and emphasize their gains rather than their losses. They are able to reach out to others, to recruit those who can help them in their journey, and to offer love and support to others. They face life's challenges with confidence and maintain a vision of hope for the future.

In our own research, we found compelling evidence for personal resilience among family members. In fact, 86 percent of our participants reported some positive consequences as a result of the mental illness in their families. Some of these included:

- personal growth and development, such as increased tolerance, empathy, compassion, and understanding;

- better self-concept, including a sense of greater strength, discipline, and personal stability;

- enhanced skills for coping with the mental illness and other challenges;

- significant contributions to other families and to society;

- effective advocacy for improvements in the mental health system;

- better family and social life, such as special closeness within their family;

- healthier perspective and priorities, such as a clearer sense of what is important; and

- greater appreciation of life and mental health.

Here are two voices that affirm the potential for personal resilience under difficult circumstances. The first family member has a parent with mental illness; the second is a sibling:

I can now say that, like that old aluminum foil ad, I am "oven-tempered for flexible strength." I'm coming out of a household rocked by mental illness, alcoholism, and divorce. I grew up much too quickly. Yet I'm not hiding from my personal problems. I'm dealing with them, one at a time. And I'm succeeding, making great progress.

It's made me more compassionate toward those who don't have the abilities I have. I've become more cognizant of my blessings. I feel a responsibility to become involved with the mental health movement in some way, to improve the care the mentally ill receive. It's definitely helped us to realize our abilities and talents, how precious life is.

At the same time, resilience never occurs in isolation; it is universally accompanied by feelings of loss and demoralization. In the words of one family member, "Any increased sensitivity to others or any other 'side effects' would be traded in an eyeblink for a healthy relative."

MILEPOSTS

In completing the second leg of your journey, you've reached the following mileposts:

- appreciation of your special vulnerability as a young family member;

- insight into the many ways mental illness has affected your life inside and outside your family circle; and

- awareness of your potential for a resilient response to a catastrophic family event.

With these mileposts, you have begun the process of accepting what you may have lost during your childhood and adolescence. At the same time, you can acknowledge what you may have gained—an opportunity to understand your experiences, to mourn your losses, to achieve resolution, and to savor your present. You may also begin to see yourself in a new light, as someone who has confronted the past with courage and developed some uncommon qualities along the way.

Now you're ready to shift from your past to your present, continuing to name and tame the SaC Syndrome. During the third leg, you'll explore the legacy of your early experiences for your current life and learn how these experiences continue to influence your thoughts, feelings, and behavior.

Chapter 4

REFLECTING ON
YOUR CURRENT LIFE

❦

*I have spent the last twenty-five years trying to find confidence,
love, and acceptance. I am extremely sensitive and weep easily. I
avoid intimacy but crave it desperately. I want more friends but
fear to trust. I took on a role of peacemaker at a young age and developed some exceptional coping skills—problem solving, sooth-
ing, getting along with difficult people, and intellectual searching.
I am a doer and a fixer but paid a price.*

I N RESPONDING TO our survey, this multigenerational family member wrote that she's still working through her pain, even though
decades have passed. In her view, the mental illness of her relatives
changed her entire life. As a family member yourself, you may feel that
mental illness has been the overarching event of your life, coloring your
childhood and adolescence and reverberating through the years to follow.

Perhaps you've also shared this woman's search for self-acceptance
and the approval of others, or her problems with intimacy and trust. At
the same time, you may have developed some impressive coping skills
that allowed you to meet the needs of others inside and outside your
family.

LANDMARKS

In this chapter, we continue to chart your journey as a family member, focusing now on the adult portion. You've already learned about the impact of mental illness on your family and on your early years. In this third leg, you'll shift from the past to your current life. This leg includes three major landmarks.

First, we'll examine the developmental tasks of adulthood, which can also be interrupted, postponed, or canceled by the mental illness in your family. Thus, in addition to the unfinished business of your childhood, you may carry some residue from your adult years.

Second, you'll learn how the mental illness was carried on as a legacy that continues to influence your life in unknown ways. This legacy is likely to permeate all the crawl spaces of your life, imprinting your feelings about yourself and your family, your educational and career plans, your relationships with others, and even your view of the world.

Finally, you'll see how your early experience with mental illness continues to affect your present thoughts, feelings, and behaviors, and how old wounds may surface, often without your awareness.

DEVELOPMENTAL TASKS OF ADULTHOOD

In the last chapter, we considered the developmental tasks of early childhood, middle childhood, and adolescence. We'll now examine the tasks of young, middle, and late adulthood.

Young Adulthood

During young adulthood, we usually complete our separation from our family. Following resolution of the personal, interpersonal, and vocational issues of adolescence, we're ready to make more sustained commitments to other people and to our career. Important tasks of this early phase of adulthood involve:

- intimacy, as we form close relationships with partners;
- marriage, as we formalize our long-term commitment;

- parenthood, as we contribute to the continuity of our family and of our species; and

- vocational accomplishments, as we establish and build our career.

As a family member, you may find all of these developmental tasks have been affected. You may avoid intimacy to prevent further losses, reconsider marriage in light of your troubled family history, weigh the genetic risks of mental illness as you consider having children, and find your career choices influenced by your earlier encounter with mental illness. The following man shares some of these concerns:

> I feel like I've lost most of the people I care about. As an adult, I've found intimacy and sexual relationships extremely difficult. I find it difficult to talk to people about my family and feel like a perpetual outsider. I'm still ashamed and self-critical. I tend to deal with emotionally threatening situations by withdrawing. I'm afraid of having children.

Middle Adulthood

Middle adulthood is often a transitional period, characterized both by increased stress and by an opportunity for constructive change and renewal. During midlife, individuals frequently reevaluate their earlier commitments, modifying these commitments in response to changing circumstances. The central tasks of middle adulthood typically include:

- renegotiation of earlier personal, interpersonal, and vocational commitments; and

- launching of children, with a return to a narrower family structure.

During this phase, you may again find your developmental agenda disrupted by the mental illness in your family. You may have difficulty balancing your responsibilities to your two families (your original family and your spouse and children), may defer your midlife opportunity to close the gap between former dreams and current achievements, and may reconsider your earlier decision to postpone or avoid marriage or child rearing. If you serve as a caregiver at midlife, you may share this woman's sense of an "awesome challenge":

> I have had to seek permanent legal guardianship of the person and the property to protect my mother and to make decisions about her medication. It is an awesome challenge to be faced with this role at my age and stage of life. I hope there will be a time when I will not be so involved in my mother's care—a time to pull away. It is so much responsibility.

Late Adulthood

Late adulthood brings a new set of challenges and opportunities for most of us. During this phase we often adapt to more restricted vocational, financial, and social circumstances. We also confront the imminence of our own mortality and the need to attain a sense of meaning and coherence in our lives. This phase of development also brings an opportunity for a period of successful aging that is marked by growth, vitality, and creativity. Important tasks during late adulthood include:

- grandparenthood, which offers continuity with past and future generations;

- retirement, as we relinquish the structure, challenges, and satisfactions of our career;

- financial security during a period of potentially depleted resources;

- loss of intimate relationships, as our companions face illness and death;

- personal illness and mortality, as we deal with similar issues ourselves; and

- life review, as we search for a sense of order and meaning in our lives.

During late adulthood, you may serve as a caregiver or guardian for your relative. With these added responsibilities, you may have little energy remaining for the uncluttered joys of retirement and grandchildren or for your own life review. If you have avoided marriage or childbearing, you may experience a sense of barrenness in later years. In addition, late adulthood is a period of loss and impending loss of intimate relationships. Those losses may be heightened by the losses that accompany the mental illness of a beloved sibling or parent.

The next family member has spent many decades coming to terms with the legacy of his family circumstances. Now in his fifties, he has not yet married, although he remains in a long-term relationship:

> My sister is also struggling to overcome the effects of our troubled family. She has worked hard to achieve a successful career and financial security. Yet, despite counseling, unresolved issues have blocked her from marrying and enjoying ongoing, intimate relationships. With no children expected, our family line appears to be ending.

All of these developmental phases of adulthood are overcast by your legacy as a family member, which consists of a personal legacy, an occupational legacy, an interpersonal legacy, and a family legacy. Together, they comprise the SaC Syndrome in adulthood.

YOUR PERSONAL LEGACY

The mental illness of a close relative has an especially devastating impact on the personal lives of family members, whose internal landscape may resemble an emotional minefield. The personal legacy evolves during your childhood and adolescence and is carried into adulthood, marking all of the developmental phases and their accompanying tasks. Your personal legacy may include:

- problems with identity and self-esteem, which may leave you unsure of yourself and uneasily dependent on the approval of others;

- residue from your earlier coping strategies, such as dissociation and psychic numbing;

- excessive needs for perfectionism and control to compensate for your chaotic and unpredictable family situation; and

- personal mental health concerns.

Listen as the following family member describes his personal legacy:

I believe it has hardened me. I can't seem to love myself. I take care of others, but when I try to take care of me, I fail. I have become an angry person. A person who is afraid not to be liked by others. A person who fears close relationships but longs for them daily. A person who is afraid of change but who longs for adventure.

Identity and Self-Esteem

All children and adolescents cope with identity issues, as they seek to discover who they are and how they fit into the grand scheme of things. For many family members, these issues are infinitely more complex. As a family member yourself, your emerging sense of identity may have been colored by the stigma that surrounds mental illness, by your relative's psychotic symptoms, by your family disruption, and by concerns about your own mental health. Each of these factors can contribute to a weak or conflicted sense of adult identity, as noted by 63 percent of our survey participants. One sibling wrote about her adolescent struggles: "Life seemed so unpredictable, so out of control. I was trying to find my place in the world, and my brother disrupted this world."

Identity issues take on a special intensity in certain relationships. For example, you may have identified with a parent or older sibling who had mental illness and internalized some unhealthy experiences and concerns. Likewise, twinship is likely to intensify all aspects of the sibling relationship, particularly when one twin develops a mental illness. One well twin shared some of her experiences with us. Like most twins, she and her sister were very close as they were growing up. They were roommates in college when her sister developed the symptoms of schizophrenia that would result in repeated hospitalizations. She talks about some of her experiences:

> It is especially difficult to look exactly like someone who behaves in ways that I would never dream of. And stigma is much harder to deal with because we are fused together in people's minds. Survivor's guilt is very common among well twins. I have a strong sense of responsibility regarding my sister. Given the close nature of the twin bond, the identical twin is a likely candidate for caregiving responsibilities.

With respect to identity, she wrote of her fear of developing mental illness herself and her anxiety when others confuse her with her sister or assume she has mental illness simply because her sister does. In her words, "I am already watching myself like a hawk for any signs of a nervous breakdown. I don't need others to add to this."

In addition to identity problems, your self-esteem may have suffered as a result of your early experiences. In fact, 75 percent of our survey participants reported low-self esteem as a consequence of their encounter with mental illness. The concept of the "looking-glass self" emphasizes the role of other people's appraisals in the development of self-esteem among children. Children who receive positive appraisals are likely to develop healthy regard for themselves, to believe in their own capabilities, and to expect that they will succeed.

It is sometimes difficult for a parent who is struggling with mental illness to provide affirmation for a child. If you have not received such affirmation during your childhood, you may have little confidence in your ability as an adult. At the same time, like family members everywhere, your self-esteem was probably eroded by the stigma surrounding mental illness. Even if you have an impressive record of accomplishment, you may worry that your pattern of success will crumble, allowing others to discover the "truth" about you. This sibling talks about the impact of her sister's mental illness on her own self-concept:

> The presence of this illness in my life had translated into low self-esteem and a pervasive sense of shame. I was extremely sensitive to what others thought of me, ready to read in to

their comments that they thought I was crazy, or at least inappropriate.

Psychic Numbing

As we've discussed, to protect yourself as a child, you may have partially cut off painful memories, images, or feelings through dissociation. Or perhaps you attempted to shut down your emotional life through psychic numbing, as was the case with 70 percent of our participants. In the words of one family member, "I lost the ability to feel for so many years. It was the only way I could protect myself and survive. It was more than I could handle." Although these defensive maneuvers may have diminished your pain in the past, they carry a high price in the present. As an adult, you may have had difficulty reversing your emotional paralysis and find yourself imprisoned in an emotional desert, as was the case for this multigenerational family member:

> I shut down emotionally sometime in my youth and this carried over into my adulthood. I didn't know how to relate to other people, especially women, beyond the superficial. I have become less human, less trusting, less vulnerable, more of a mechanical man who is hollow inside. It has put my life on emotional hold for twenty years.

Perfectionism and Control

Family members often talk about their feelings of helplessness and insecurity. In the words of a multigenerational family member, "My whole life was changed. Living with fear—fear that I would lose control and become ill, fear that my children would have it, fear of the unexpected." Such feelings may leave young family members with an inordinate need for perfectionism and control as adults (63 percent of our participants reported a need to be perfect). As an adult, you too may live with a sense of impending doom that can be kept at bay only by rigorous efforts to maintain structure and control.

These problems may be intensified if as a child you felt responsible for your relative's symptoms or relapses, which can engender a magical sense of power. During her childhood, this woman experienced an "unstable feeling" because she never knew when her father might relapse:

> The burden of thinking anything I do or any mistake I make might result in the "craziness" has made me feel insecure unless I can control the situation. It has made me feel overly responsible for others, that I have an exaggerated power to cause others' behavior.

Personal Mental Health Concerns

Like other family members, you may experience two kinds of mental health concerns: fear of developing serious mental illness yourself and worry about other mental health problems. Although your risk of developing serious mental illness is relatively low, this fear may cast a long shadow over your own life and intensify your feelings of helplessness. Even after you have passed the late-adolescent and early-adulthood period of greatest risk, you may continue to experience anxiety about your own mental health.

Your anxiety may be heightened by the powerful subjective burden experienced by family members. A majority of our survey participants reported feelings of helplessness and hopelessness and of personal depression. Sometimes these family members described an undercurrent of depression that surfaced with more intensity in response to difficult life events. Other family members reported deeper feelings of demoralization that undermined their effectiveness and enjoyment of life:

> My mother was hospitalized a total of thirty-three times in her life. I've probably always had a degree of depression as a result of her mental illness. When my father died, I suffered a major depression and went into therapy myself. On the positive side, I became a psychologist as a result of her illness, and I bring empathy and understanding to my work.

Your Occupational Legacy

Many adult siblings and offspring report that their experience with mental illness has had a major impact on their educational and career plans. As a family member, you may have experienced some of the following:

- an impact on your career choices, as you either duplicate or flee from your earlier caregiving role;

- poor performance in your career, which may seem insignificant compared to your family drama;

- overinvolvement in your career to avoid family problems; and

- a sense of unfulfilled career potential, which may compound your lifetime feelings of loss.

The next family member comes from a large family that includes two siblings with mental illness. He talks about his choice of a teaching career:

> My sister has been in and out of state hospitals for her whole life. You had to have a thick skin to handle this. I tended to be an overachiever because I didn't want to add to the pain in our house. I'm a teacher. My oldest brother is also a teacher. We have gone toward human services like magnets because we can handle all this.

Although this man feels his career has benefited from his early experiences, others may not be so fortunate. Another family member told us: "I had completely lost the thread of my own life."

Career Choices

As a family member, your career choice may have been affected in two directions. On one hand, you may have been drawn to a career in caregiving, which offers an accustomed and satisfying role. In our research, many family members remarked on the link between their early exposure to mental illness and their choice of a caregiving career in the fields of education, health care, or mental health:

I think my childhood experience led me into the mental health field because of my compassion for the people and their families and because I am comfortable with a certain amount of "craziness." It has made me very empathic and understanding. And it has forced me personally to get into counseling and deal with my issues.

On the other hand, you may have avoided careers that duplicated your earlier caregiving responsibilities, preferring to work in less familiar territory. In either case, your earlier encounter with mental illness has had an impact on your choice of a career.

Poor Career Performance

We spoke earlier about the disruptive force of mental illness in your family and its negative consequences for your academic life. This force may continue to drain energy needed to establish and further your career. As he was struggling to begin a career, for example, one family member felt that "most of the 'real' news in my life centered around the mental illness of my family members." Similarly, the next sibling talks about the adverse impact of her family situation on her career:

I was looking for a job and had absolutely no self-confidence. I began to be overcome by a debilitating depression. It was as if I were conditioned to react to family crises and couldn't find the energy to invest in my own life. Each time a hospitalization came up, I went into a crisis mode, visiting the hospital and doing what was necessary. Between crises I went into a funk, like a soldier weary of battle.

Overinvolvement in a Career

Sometimes the accumulated residue of mental illness in your family may loom as a specter that threatens to overwhelm and sabotage your own life. Under these circumstances, you may execute a flight from your troubled family and your own unresolved issues, submerging yourself in a career to block out your anguish. In the absence of resolution, however, these issues may surface later in life with an intensity that commands attention.

Rex talks about his own flight from his troubled family, as he moved into college, graduate school, and a career. His brother's death dismantled the fragile structure he had erected:

> After David's suicide, part of me said, "I quit. What's the point of it all?" The linear progression—of college, engineering work, Air Force piloting, graduate school, flight work— now changed. Increasingly I lost an earlier optimistic attitude and sense of direction. It was as if we were all passengers on a dangerous renegade train.

Sense of Unfulfilled Potential

The mental illness in your family may preclude you from establishing a meaningful and satisfying career at all. A recurrent theme among adult siblings and offspring is the burnout and exhaustion that result from the mental illness in their families. This man reflects on the personal price he has paid for his encounter with his mother's mental illness:

> I feel a powerful sense of loss for many ill-advised decisions I made about my education and career in the past fifteen years, a powerful sense of regret for lost opportunities. I'm left with a great deal of shame associated with my feeling that I haven't lived up to the promise I once exhibited.

Along with 64 percent of our participants, you too may share this family member's sense of unfulfilled potential. Even when your accomplishments have been impressive, you may be acutely aware of your real or perceived shortcomings and of your unrealized hopes and dreams. As one man declared, "My accomplishments began to seem meaningless as I helplessly watched my family members become enveloped with mental illness."

YOUR INTERPERSONAL LEGACY

Through your searing encounter with mental illness, you probably developed some qualities that make you a valued and sensitive friend. Along with other resilient family members, you may have become a better and stronger person—more tolerant, empathic, and compassionate. And your early experiences may have cultivated some unusual gifts. One family member wrote: "After a lifetime of tuning in to how things were with my mother, I have radar that can tune in to others' moods, to read between the lines."

At the same time, family members often tell us they have significant problems in their adult relationships. Many of their difficulties result from the continuation of earlier patterns that have become maladaptive in the present. Even if you are one of the resilient family members we've discussed, your resilience may carry a high psychological price. For example, in your effort to cope with your painful reality, you may have shut down emotionally, avoided close relationships, become precariously dependent on the approval of others, or channeled energy into your career. All of these strategies can undermine your relationships with your family, friends, and even coworkers.

Not surprisingly, these patterns can also undermine your capacity for intimate relationships. In response to your intense feelings of anguish and loss, for instance, you may develop a shell that shields you from further pain. Unfortunately, this protective shell may limit your capacity for close and sustained relationships, and may prevent you from communicating openly with others. In the words of one family member, "If I opened my mouth, some of the terror inside might come spilling out."

In connection with your interpersonal legacy, you may have experienced some of the following:

- a sense of social alienation and isolation, as the stigma surrounding mental illness pervades your own life;

- continuation of maladaptive patterns, which may undermine close relationships in the present;

- problems with trust and intimacy, which may impair the relationships you do establish; and

- reluctance to make a long-term commitment.

Social Alienation and Isolation

Family members often experience a sense of social alienation and isolation, as did 61 percent of our participants. Early researchers described the social patterns of families who had a member with mental illness as similar to those of minority groups, including feelings of marginality, social distance, concealment, hypersensitivity, and underprivilege. One woman noted that she and her brother had both been deeply affected by their mother's mental illness. With the assistance of personal counseling, she eventually learned to feel more comfortable and secure around other people. But her brother remains "completely withdrawn, a middle-aged man with no friends or relationships."

Maladaptive Patterns

As a young family member, you shared in the subjective and objective burden of your family. You also developed strategies to cope with this burden. These early experiences may leave a residue of maladaptive responses and patterns that undermine your relationships in the present, often with little awareness on your part. For example, you may carry a fear of rejection that deters you from establishing close relationships. If you also suffer from low self-esteem, when you do establish relationships, you may choose unsuitable partners. As one woman wrote, "I'm afraid people will reject me. I've been looking for love in inappropriate people and ways."

Another maladaptive pattern is an excessive need to please others. Along with many other family members, as a child you may have minimized your own needs in your effort to assist your family. As you matured, this pattern may have become entrenched, forever compelling you to meet the needs of others at your own expense. As one sibling wrote, "I feel that I've denied my needs, interests, and goals. I have a hard time taking steps to focus on myself, making myself happy."

A third pattern is the tendency of family members to continue a caregiving role in later relationships. If you pursue a caregiving role in your adult relationships, you face the dual risks of choosing a troubled partner who needs your ministrations or of alienating someone who prefers not to be parented. Neither offers a good foundation for a mature relationship.

This family member assumed a caregiving role early in life, which has influenced his career choice as well as his adult relationships:

> I have married someone who needs to be taken care of and I can't seem to open up to people, no matter how I try. I'm afraid of being hurt. As a career, guess what—I'm a social worker.

Trust and Intimacy

If you have been exposed to mental illness during your early years, you may be particularly vulnerable to problems with trust and intimacy as an adult. Here is one woman's account:

> My manic mother, with my father's complicity, would go on enormous spending sprees—buy literally housefuls of furniture in one day, buy lavish gifts. Not surprisingly, they were always in debt; our furniture would get repossessed. They would pawn presents they gave us—a feast/famine pattern. I liked all the presents, but felt betrayed when they were taken back. Adults were not to be trusted.

Another family member talks about his teenage years with a brother and sister who both had mental illness. His words convey a sense of betrayal and a determination to avoid being hurt in the future:

> I remember at eighteen, I swore I would never trust anyone for the rest of my life. I went through a lot of therapy. I never had friends over and never told anyone that my brother and sister were psychotic. I was terribly ashamed of their illness. I was continually angry. I learned to develop a complete wall mentally to protect myself.

An inability to trust and a fear of abandonment may lead to avoidance of intimacy altogether. This strategy offers protection from hurtful or unhealthy relationships, but at the intolerable price of enduring loneliness. As one woman wrote, "I never put myself in a position of needing anyone, because people I needed were never available. I had trouble trusting others and so became self-sufficient."

Long-Term Commitment

These problems with trust and intimacy are likely to affect your willingness and capacity to make an enduring commitment. Feelings of love may coexist with fears of abandonment and rejection, creating intense conflict. The SaC Syndrome has colored this sibling's entire life:

> I have not had a relationship with a woman longer than one year. I withdrew socially, became very introverted, and had low self-esteem. I was trying to achieve but it felt like I was working on only one or two cylinders out of four. Seeing my brother homeless, learning that it's probably futile for me to do anything.

YOUR FAMILY LEGACY

Family psychologists speak of our two families: the "family of origin" in which we grew up and the "family of procreation" that includes our spouse and children. Balancing the needs of these two families is challenging for everyone, at least sometimes. But there are special challenges for adult siblings and offspring who have a relative with mental illness. As a family member yourself, you may have experienced problems centering on:

- your marriage;
- your children;
- your caregiving responsibilities; and
- your commitments to yourself and your two families.

In our mobile society, many adults live far from their families of origin. This geographic distance poses particular problems for family members. For example, in the case of siblings whose aging parents have served as primary caregivers for their adult son or daughter with mental illness, there may be no easy way to provide continuity of caregiving:

> My brother, who is diagnosed with schizophrenia, lives in Florida near our parents, who are both now turning eighty. I live a thousand miles away in Maine. I have a sister who lives in California. Over the years, my brother has received a lot of support from Mom and Dad. When they die, what do my sister and I do? What are our responsibilities? It's a deeply troubling question that cannot easily be avoided.

Marriage

We've described an interpersonal legacy marked by problems with trust and intimacy, by ambivalent and conflicted relationships, and by reluctance to make a sustained commitment. In turn, these problems may affect your marital experience. For example, you may have attempted to escape from your difficult family situation by entering into marriage before you had the maturity to make a constructive choice of partners or had resolved your personal issues. One woman wrote: "I spent a lifetime in fantasy, waiting for my knight in shining armor to save me from all of this. And I clung to the very first person who came into my life—I married my first boyfriend."

Marriages established under such circumstances are clearly at risk for early dissolution:

> At seventeen, I married—relieved to get away. By twenty-one, I had two children and threw myself into their care. I am divorced and not very trusting of people, have only a few close friends. I still fear relying on others and am independent beyond what is comfortable.

Possibly you delayed or avoided marriage as a result of your personal and interpersonal legacy. In fact, in our research, over one-third of our participants had remained single. Compare this to the 10 percent that the Census Bureau estimates will never marry. One man in his mid-forties wrote: "I hope I am prepared for a more fulfilling relationship than those

I have experienced in the past. It has taken me time to emotionally understand concepts such as trust, vulnerability, and personal boundaries."

If you do marry, you may find you are duplicating unhealthy patterns
from the past. A family member talked about the adverse impact of her
mother's mental illness on her first marriage: "I reproduced what I
learned from my mother—rant, rave, fly around." Speaking from experience, another woman offered this advice: "Resolve your own issues and
be sensitive to their impact on adult relationships."

As a child, you probably experienced profound feelings of loss for
your own childhood and for your family. In compensation, you may have
a fervent need to create a new and more perfect family in the present. Although this need is likely to foster a strong commitment to marriage and
parenthood, you may strive for a degree of "togetherness" that alienates a
partner with a reasonable need for independence and undermines the au-
tonomy of your children.

Children

The SaC Syndrome also affects your parenting. Indeed, your early encounter with mental illness may deter you from having children altogether. Still reeling from the mental illness of your relative and fearful of
the potential for mental illness in another generation, you may choose to
avoid the risk of another trauma. The next sibling considers this option:

> I will probably never have children. I have learned to deal
> with my sister's illness, but I don't think I could deal with it
> happening to my own child. How do you deal with raising a
> normal, healthy, happy child, only to helplessly watch the fu-
> ture fall apart? The pain experienced by a parent must be
> much greater than that of a sibling.

If you do choose to become a parent, you may find your early experience shadows your parenthood. Family members often express concern
about the risk of mental illness in their own children and may assume a
state of vigilance that heightens anxiety within their family. In fact, although there is a slightly increased risk of developing mental illness
among the grandchildren, nieces, and nephews of people with mental ill-

ness, the risk is actually quite low. Nevertheless, you may share the concern of a woman who wrote, "I was afraid to have children because I had a fear that they might be like my dad."

Once they become parents, family members may face additional problems. Our own parenting is strongly influenced by our early family experience. Mothers and fathers serve as essential models and objects of identification. Often with little awareness, we internalize their values and attitudes, their approach to discipline, their coping strategies, and their modes of communication. Even if we have sworn to avoid duplicating the mistakes of our parents, when we become parents ourselves we may find ourselves repeating their words and deeds.

Of greater concern, our own parenting may suffer if our role models are inadequate, as they were for this family member:

> I had a problem with my oldest son. I was going to love him like my mother never loved me. But I was suffocating my child—I was driving him away from me. I had to learn to start becoming an effective parent, something I hadn't learned while growing up. My only role model was a schizophrenic mother.

Caregiving

Over the course of your life, you may serve as a caregiver or informal case manager for your relative. If you are a primary caregiver who resides with your relative, your responsibilities may place you at risk for exhaustion and burnout. Family members who are not primary caregivers sometimes function as informal case managers on an as-needed basis, advocating for their relatives, handling crises, securing needed services, and consulting with professional caregivers. If you serve in either of these roles, you may feel you have undertaken an unanticipated second career.

Even during periods of relative calm, you may maintain a crisis mode, awaiting the next urgent phone call. If the crisis imposes demands that conflict with your obligations to your own spouse and children, you may experience considerable distress, feeling that you're falling short on all fronts. You may also share the frustration of the next family member, who has always been active in her mother's treatment:

The biggest problem I have had is getting people to listen to me, to take seriously what I had to say about my mother. To understand that I know her better than anyone because of having lived with her so long with this illness.

Even if you're not currently involved in caregiving, you may worry about your future responsibilities in the face of an unrelenting illness. Almost all of our survey participants—94 percent—shared the sense of lifetime responsibility, as this sibling conveys:

I worry about the present and future. I am concerned about my parents and the burdens they have undergone in helping my sister. I worry about myself, the choices I can and will make. I have mixed feelings about whether I can and want to be a caregiver. I worry about a grim future when our parents die.

Family members who assume roles as primary caregivers or informal case managers must often deal with the legal system as well as the mental health system. If you are a caregiver, for example, you may need to become familiar with the regulations governing involuntary commitment in your state, with estate planning that can ensure continuity of caregiving, and with procedures for establishing medical and financial powers of attorney. The advice of an attorney who specializes in mental health law and estate planning can be invaluable under these circumstances.

You may also wish to contact NAMI (the information is in Appendix A) to obtain information about the Planned Lifetime Assistance Network (PLAN), which can provide continuity of care for your relative. The program is based on an individualized written plan that specifies the supplementary benefits to be provided to your relative and the financial means (usually a type of trust) to pay for the service.

Balancing Commitments

Almost universally, family members struggle to balance their own needs with those of their families and to reach an equitable arrangement that honors all of their commitments. In our survey, 84 percent of the participants expressed this concern. There is no easy solution to a dilemma that sometimes places personal and family commitments in painful opposition. Even if you are relatively young and unencumbered by responsibilities in the present, you may worry about your responsibilities in an uncertain future:

> As a father figure I feel very confused about my responsibilities to my sister. I live in fear of having my life interrupted periodically, especially after my parents are no longer able to care for her.

Particularly as a young adult, in your quest for self-preservation you may have attempted to place as much psychological and geographical distance as possible between yourself and your family. This disengagement is often accompanied by intense feelings of guilt for abandoning a family that continues to labor under the onus of mental illness. In the words of one man, "I sought my first job as far away as I could get. This further deepened my feelings of guilt but was essential so I didn't end up psychotic myself."

In addition to feelings of guilt, a path of disengagement may deprive you of your family's love and support. Even when your family connection has been broken, the emotional residue is likely to remain for a lifetime. Some family members may reengage with their family of origin after they have established a secure base outside their family or in response to a family crisis. In fact, we often hear from family members who have assumed a more active role in caregiving or advocacy for their relative after they have established a family of their own. But whatever your current situation, along with so many family members you are likely to struggle for a lifetime to find a comfortable balance.

MILEPOSTS

You've now completed the third leg of your journey and achieved the following mileposts:

- knowledge of the developmental tasks of adulthood, which may have been interrupted by the mental illness in your family, thus adding to your unfinished business;

- understanding of the personal meaning of mental illness for your adulthood, including your personal, occupational, inter-personal, and family legacy; and

- insight into the impact of your early experience with mental illness on your present thoughts, feelings, and behavior.

At this juncture you have largely named your SaC Syndrome. Beginning with the next leg of your journey, we'll focus more on the taming part of the process. As you tame your earlier experiences, they will lose their power over your life.

Chapter 5

RESOLVING YOUR LEGACY

༄

*The first support-group meeting changed my life. The group has
been like a beacon, providing me with information, support, and
understanding. I am learning to set limits, to say no, to live apart,
to have a happy, well-adjusted life—and not to feel guilty about it.
I still feel responsible for "saving" my family, but it is set within
realistic perimeters. Most important, I know that I am not alone in
this.*

WHEN THIS WOMAN was growing up, she always looked up to
her brother, who was almost like a third parent to her. He
was viewed as a genius by her family; the entire family was
devastated by his mental illness. As a college student, she was confused
and troubled by the symptoms of her brother's illness. She contacted a
support group in her area, which has since served as an essential resource
and sanctuary for her.

During this leg of your journey we'll explore support groups and
other resources that can meet your needs. Like many other family members, you may find that a support group offers you a protected forum for
resolving your emotional burden, for obtaining essential information, for
developing realistic expectations, and for a finding a comfortable balance
in your life.

The naming of your SaC Syndrome is now largely complete. You've learned about the disruptive effects of mental illness on your family system, about your special vulnerability as a young family member, and about the legacy you've carried as an adult. It's time to proceed to the taming part of the process.

Many terms can be applied to this process, but none really satisfactorily. We've been using the term *resolution,* which implies an ability to make something understandable or to deal with it successfully. Certainly, resolution is involved. We can also talk about *acceptance,* which involves recognizing the meaning of the mental illness and managing to endure its presence in your life. So acceptance is both a cognitive and an emotional process, as you gain better understanding of the personal meaning of mental illness and as you work through your emotional burden and grieve your losses. In addition, we can speak about *adaptation,* which refers to adjustment or accommodation to your family circumstances. Again, adaptation is clearly part of your own process.

Thus, the taming of the SaC Syndrome involves resolution, acceptance, and adaptation. But this is a lifelong process for you, one that is always incomplete. Resolution is accompanied by a residue of chronic sorrow. Acceptance is coupled with an enduring sense of disbelief that leaves you forever wondering how mental illness could have struck your family. And adaptation to your family circumstances invariably leaves some unfinished business. A smaller legacy perhaps; but a legacy nonetheless.

The taming process is at the center of the fourth leg of your journey of hope and healing. As we'll discuss, many factors influence your process of adaptation, including your personal and family circumstances and your larger social world. There are also many possible outcomes—both positive and negative—for you, for your relative, and for your family. Indeed, over a lifetime the most likely course is one that includes both positive and negative consequences for all of you. The following family member traces her own journey with an admired older sister who developed schizophrenia as a teenager:

> I wanted to be just like my big sister. Then I realized that there was something really wrong with her—and my point of reference was gone. It took me so long to figure out what was

normal and good. I felt so bad for her. I was sure I was going to grow up and be a psychiatrist and rescue her.

Twenty years later, my sister is living an incredibly normal life. She is happily married and holding a good computer job. There really is hope! She takes medication and is able to keep all the voices under control. Our relationship is great—we have the same sister feelings we had before her illness.

LANDMARKS

This leg of your journey includes three significant landmarks. First, we'll explore your adaptation process, including the phases of adaptation and the factors that can affect the process.

Second, we'll discuss your essential needs as a family member, including your needs for information, skills, support, and resolution of your emotional burden.

Finally, we'll examine some resources that can facilitate your adaptation process and meet your needs.

At the end of this leg, the taming part of your process will be well under way.

PHASES OF ADAPTATION

One way of looking at your process of adaptation is in terms of various phases or stages. In fact, almost all of our survey participants felt they had progressed through a series of stages as they adapted to the mental illness in their family. Like these family members, your own adaptation process is likely to conform to the three-stage structure used to describe the grieving process in the case of biological death and other significant losses:

- avoidance, which is characterized by feelings of shock, denial, and disbelief;

- confrontation, which is characterized by intense feelings of grief, loss, anger, helplessness, depression, and guilt; and

- resolution, which is characterized by understanding and acceptance and by reinvestment of energy in your own life.

We'll briefly examine each of these phases, although it's important to remember that there's no single pattern of adaptation for all family members. Your own adaptation process may vary from this general pattern. For example, some family members don't appear to experience denial during their initial encounter with mental illness, but are instantly and fully aware of the illness. Others seem to remain forever embedded in the confrontation phase and consumed by their feelings of loss and grief. And—as you undoubtedly know from experience—you're more likely to move back and forth among these phases than to progress smoothly through them, and to experience a degree of chronic sorrow than to reach a tranquil sea of acceptance. Nevertheless, many family members do seem to undergo these phases, which may help you understand your own journey.

Your Initial Encounter

When individuals first encounter their relative's mental illness, they often experience feelings of shock, denial, and confusion. In fact, their initial response is often a paralyzing sense of disbelief. If you are like most family members, at the onset you had little understanding of mental illness or its meaning for your family. During this phase, denial may serve as a defense mechanism that protects you from the full force of this catastrophic event. A sibling talks about the role of denial in her adaptation process:

> Denial was the longest stage. In some ways denial was helpful.
> I was able to get on with my life in high school, not realizing
> that my brother's illness was serious. As an adult, I continued
> to run away from the situation. It was obviously not a healthy
> response, but I had my own separate issues.

As your feelings of disbelief diminish and you proceed to the confrontation phase, you may feel you're in the midst of an emotional holocaust.

Confrontation

During the confrontation phase, you may experience a range of powerful emotions, including grief, anger, guilt, and despair. Perhaps, like this woman, you tried to avoid your family's painful reality, leaving it to fester below the surface:

> I spent years hiding from my pain. It is difficult to let hurt flow; I want to continue to push it down. But I know that I can't be released from the pain until I acknowledge it, and let myself feel it. Only then can I grow from it. It will probably be a lifelong process for me.

Whatever your initial reaction to the mental illness, and however earnestly others attempted to protect you, eventually you did feel the full force of this disruptive family event. Especially at the onset of the confrontation phase, you may suffer periodic emotional firestorms that consume your energy and interfere with ongoing activities. In fact, many family members are subject to intense distress—chronic sorrow—on a long-term basis in response to crises, relapses, or other emotional triggers. In the words of one man, "From time to time I feel pretty depressed, while at other times I get overwhelmed and feel paralyzed."

Resolution

During the resolution phase, you'll experience the gradual decline of the intense feelings experienced earlier. As you confront the full impact of mental illness, you gradually work through your painful emotions and can place the mental illness in perspective, as a single event in your life. Although your loss is not forgotten, you're now able to reinvest your emotional energy in new relationships and activities.

Almost universally, however, family members find their adaptation process a slow, difficult, and uneven process. There is no quick and painless route:

> My sister became ill when I was seventeen. It was devastating. I kept waiting for my sister to get better. I continued to be hurt by her illness. Finally, after at least ten years, I realized

she will not get better. This actually was helpful, the painful acceptance.

Traumatic and Posttraumatic Reactions

In addition to these phases of adaptation, you are at risk for a traumatic reaction that can cause intense emotional and physical distress, or even for a posttraumatic reaction that can affect you for many years. If you were traumatized by the mental illness as a young family member, you may have experienced heightened fears and anxieties, loss of pleasure in your activities, sleep-related difficulties, withdrawal and constriction, a need to retell and replay the trauma, and unwanted images and thoughts.

As we've mentioned, your earlier efforts to defend yourself from trauma may have posed additional risks of their own. For example, you may have attempted to deny your frightening reality or to replace your reality with fantasy. Perhaps you avoided thinking about the mental illness or split off painful memories, images, or emotions associated with the trauma. Here is one family member's description:

> Many of my memories of events have been lost, others are clouded; and then there are those that are finely etched in my memory. Parts of it play through my mind like a movie in slow motion. I can't recall the significant details, such as my age or the date, but I remember seemingly mundane aspects, such as what I was wearing and the print of the fabric. The physical and emotional sensations are also easily conjured up.

Family members often struggle to avoid their painful feelings so they can move on with their lives. But the price of this avoidance may be emotional flooding later in life. One family member wrote about her efforts to keep her early trauma at bay. These efforts were largely successful. She graduated from college, started a career, and obtained a master's degree. But the impact of mental illness was catching up to her, and she went through therapy at age twenty-three. Although she began to confront some of the feelings she had held inside for so long, no connection was made between these feelings and her mother's mental illness:

Then at age thirty-five, after the birth of my child and my husband's cancer, being the accomplished heroine all the while, I finally gave in emotionally. Thirty years of emotional bombing and shelling had come to an end. I couldn't run anymore.

Similarly to this family member, your early trauma and its lack of resolution may place you at risk for a posttraumatic reaction that can persist for months or years. One sibling wrote: "I felt doomed for many years." In adults, symptoms of posttraumatic reactions may include recurrent and distressing images, thoughts, dreams, or flashbacks; psychic numbing; and a range of other symptoms, such as a lack of interest in activities, a feeling of estrangement from other people, a restricted range of emotions, irritability, or difficulty concentrating. The following multigenerational family member talks about her own evocative images:

Images are also a problem. They are set off by seemingly little things—walking by a homeless person on the street, watching a cop show on television—and it's like a slide projector switches on in my head. Images—of my brother walking the icy streets as he hunts for food and a place to sleep, of my sister being handcuffed and forced into a police car—flash by, each a twist of the knife in my gut. They come unannounced. They hurt. They're hard to switch off.

As Dr. Aphrodite Matsakis discusses in her handbook for trauma survivors, you may also experience "secondary wounding" if others respond to your distress with ignorance and insensitivity. For instance, they may discount the magnitude of your trauma, blame you for your family problems, or judge you negatively because of your reactions. Thus, just as you need to heal from the original trauma, you also need to work through the secondary wounds.

In our research, we've found that these traumatic and posttraumatic experiences are not uncommon among family members, especially if they were exposed to mental illness when they were very young. Yet some family members are not traumatized by this family event. One woman said she simply experienced the mental illness as "a fact" in the larger context of her family life. It was not until she entered the world outside her family that she discovered others did not share her perception:

> It had never occurred to me that I should be adversely affected. I remember standing up in second grade and sharing the mental condition of my brother as my contribution to Show and Tell. I thought it was the most unique thing about my life and certainly better than any hamster! I still can see the awkward panic on my teacher's face as she hastily ushered me to my seat.

FACTORS AFFECTING YOUR ADAPTATION PROCESS

Many factors can influence your process of adaptation, including a wide range of personal, family, and social factors.

Personal Factors

Important personal characteristics and circumstances include:

- your age, birth order, and chronological proximity to your relative, which may affect your vulnerability and your responsibilities within your family;

- your gender, which may influence your tendency to identify with a same-sex relative;

- your role, since mental illness has different consequences for parents, spouses, siblings, and offspring;

- your own personality, physical health, and mental health;

- your living arrangements, which are likely to determine your degree of involvement in your relative's life; and

- the meaning of mental illness for your own life.

We've already talked about many of these factors; each of them can have a major impact. For example, one woman talked about her change of residence, noting "It is much more difficult for me to be available to 'rescue' my sister when she calls." The last factor—the personal meaning of the mental illness—is one of the most important. Family members universally struggle to make sense of this unanticipated family event and to place it in perspective. One family member wrote: "It has been hard for me to learn that I cannot 'fix' their pain. I can only heal my own." Another talked about her effort to come to terms with her relative's illness:

> The illness isn't you, and you are not responsible for it in your relative. You can be loving and helpful without taking the illness on as your responsibility. Sometimes the best thing you can do is to pull back a bit. Try to separate your relative from the illness and remember the really wonderful things about your relative as a person.

Family Factors

Family factors also define your experience of the SaC Syndrome. Important family factors include:

- life-cycle issues, such as the developmental tasks confronting you and your family;

- other stressful events confronting your family, such as unemployment or chronic medical problems;

- your family characteristics, including the composition of your family, their social class, their ethnic group, and their religious affiliation;

- the overall effectiveness of your family;

- the nature and quality of relationships among your family members; and

- the meaning of the mental illness for your family.

Earlier we discussed the universal dimensions of the family experience of mental illness. Your family also has unique characteristics that influence this experience, including your cultural background and religious beliefs. A multigenerational family member wrote about his cultural background: "In Japanese culture there is a restraint on expression of strong feelings and shame about mental illness. I have only recently begun to acknowledge my feelings." A sibling also emphasizes the importance of her family's ethnic-minority status: "In our dealings with the mental health system, we feel a sense of alienation. We have not met one African-American doctor or psychotherapist."

In addition, the meaning of mental illness for your family is central to your own adaptation process. For example, your family may view the illness as temporary or permanent, your relative's prospects for recovery as hopeless or hopeful, and their own burden as challenging or crushing. Similarly, your family may see themselves as helpless victims or active agents, as effective or ineffective problem solvers, and as a strong or weak family system. Thus, it is not simply the reality of mental illness that determines your family's process of adaptation. It is also their perception of the illness, of its meaning for them, and of their ability to cope with it. This family member describes her own effort to find meaning in her family circumstances:

> I wonder sometimes what our family would have been like without the presence of this illness. I am proud that through the heartaches there was a profound sense of love and commitment to each other that could not be dispelled. That is the legacy I'm going to carry on. I hope that I will always have the courage to help my sister. I am, at the same time, learning to insulate my life from her ups and downs.

Social Factors

A range of social factors affect your adaptation process, including:

- the services available for your relative, such as mental health, physical health, social, rehabilitative, vocational, and residential services; and

- the services available for you and your family, such as an educational program, support group, or professional counseling;

- the resources and supports available for your family; and

- sociocultural characteristics, such as social values, policies, attitudes, and barriers.

As we've mentioned, your family's experience of mental illness is etched by the larger social context. One sibling wrote about the stigma that pervades contemporary books, songs, and movies: "I like to read mysteries, but when I pick up a book at the store, read the jacket, and see that the book involves a 'psychotic' killer, I quickly lose interest."

Understanding Your Needs

As a family member, you have essential needs of your own. In our research, we asked adult siblings and offspring to rate the relative importance of various needs during childhood, adolescence, and adulthood. They told us their most important needs were for information about mental illness and its treatment, for skills to cope with the illness, for support for themselves, and for resolution of their emotional burden. Some family members also wanted to play a meaningful role in their relative's treatment. But others preferred less involvement; one wrote: "Give us a break."

Let's take a look at the four essential needs you share with other family members.

Information

Along with other family members, your need for information is central to your adaptation process. Indeed, you can't cope with something if you don't know what it is! For example, you need information about:

- the serious mental illness of your relative and its treatment and rehabilitation;

- the services and resources available to your family;

- the SaC Syndrome; and

- caregiving and management issues.

Affirming the importance of information, one family member has declared: "Knowledge has kept me from the depths of hopelessness." In the past, the informational needs of well children were often ignored. As the following family member asserts, however, children also have a compelling need for information:

> Make sure children are informed that this is an illness that has a name and that many people have. It has nothing to do with their actions or their parents' displeasure with them. There are treatments and medication for it, just like a heart problem. Tell them what behaviors they can expect and what to do and say if those behaviors are exhibited. Encourage them to discuss it.

Skills

As a family member, you also need certain coping skills. Later in the book we'll talk about the strategies that can assist you and your family, including the Personal Action Plan and the Family Action Plan. Both of these plans build on the following skills:

- communication skills;
- problem-solving skills;
- conflict-management skills;
- assertiveness skills;
- symptom-management skills; and
- stress-management skills.

Good communication skills are extremely important for family members. Your family needs to be able to communicate effectively among themselves, with professionals and other service providers, and with your relative. Basic communication skills include two essential elements: effective listening, which is active, nonjudgmental, responsive, and empathic; and effective expression, which is clear, complete, direct, and supportive. In addition to these general guidelines, it is important to minimize critical and hostile communication, which may increase your relative's level of stress.

Your family also needs good problem-solving and conflict-management skills, since the mental illness of your relative creates fertile ground for disagreement. Especially at the onset of the illness, your family may disagree about the nature of your relative's problems, about the probable causes, about treatment, and about symptom management. These differences may be heightened by professionals who fail to provide your family with accurate information. Good problem-solving and conflict-management skills may improve your family's ability to resolve issues with your relative, with other family members, and with service providers. When problems or conflicts involve other people, it is essential that the process take place in an atmosphere of mutual tolerance and respect.

Assertiveness is also an essential skill for family members, who need to be able to stand up for their legitimate rights, to refuse to allow others to take advantage of them, and to communicate their desires in an open, direct, and appropriate manner. Assertiveness involves meeting your own needs without violating the rights of others. In contrast, you should avoid passive strategies that meet the needs of others at your own expense and aggressive strategies that meet your own needs at the expense of others. On a long-term basis, neither of these strategies is effective. Passivity is likely to leave you angry and resentful, and aggression is likely to alienate others.

In light of the varied symptoms that may accompany serious mental illness, family members can benefit from effective symptom-management skills. For example, you may need help in handling such symptoms as hallucinations, delusions, apathy, disruptive behavior, suicidal or violent behavior, extreme mood swings, or substance abuse. We will later offer some practical suggestions.

Finally, given the universal stress and disruption that accompany a diagnosis of serious mental illness, family members need good stress-management skills. You can learn to manage stress more effectively by understanding the nature, kinds, and sources of stressors in your life, and by developing more effective strategies for managing stress, such as relaxation training and physical exercise. As one sibling wrote, "When you experience someone in a manic episode, you tense up to protect yourself. As my sister recovers, I find it difficult to relax the defenses I put up."

Support

One of your most pressing needs as a family member is for personal support. In the words of one family member, "The isolation was profound." You have three general sources of support:

- your informal support network, which consists of your nuclear family, your extended family, your friends and acquaintances, your neighbors, and your coworkers;

- your formal support network, which includes professionals and service providers, social institutions, and the government; and

- advocacy groups, such as the National Alliance for the Mentally Ill (NAMI), which offers you a large and effective organization comprised of people with mental illness, their family members and friends, and concerned professionals.

Family members often affirm the benefits of contact with other families, especially through NAMI and its network of adult siblings and offspring. These families can offer information, support, coping strategies, and opportunities for advocacy. Indeed, NAMI often serves as a life raft for family members, as this sibling affirms:

> Children and teenagers need support when there is a family member with mental illness. My mother and I joined NAMI and discovered resources for dealing with it. I have tried counselors and therapy, but no one except those with their own ill family members really understood.

Resolution of Your Emotional Burden

As a family member, you are likely to carry a profound emotional burden in response to the mental illness of your relative. Before you can move on in your life, you need to confront and work through your painful feelings. Some family members are able to resolve their emotional burden with the help of caring family and friends. Others may benefit from involvement in a support group or professional counseling. At the core of the emotional burden are feelings of grief for your own losses and those of other members of your family. One sibling wrote: "Our family has lost a great deal to this illness. I carry pain about my sister every day."

MEETING YOUR NEEDS

There are many ways you can meet your needs. First, you can reach out to others who care about you. Feelings of isolation are almost universal for family members. Once you break your silence about the mental illness in your family, given the incidence of serious mental illness, chances are you'll find other family members among your friends, neighbors, and coworkers. Open yourself to their comfort.

In addition, you can learn more about mental illness. As your knowledge increases, you'll find yourself feeling more confident and less anxious about your family situation. There are many resources available, including some excellent books and videotapes (see Appendix A). You can also benefit from community organizations, lectures and workshops, and perhaps college psychology classes. As we hear repeatedly from family members, knowledge is empowering! One family member wrote: "Books, literature, tapes, and conferences have provided inspiration and hope and valuable information about mental illness."

You may also benefit from involvement in a specialized support group for adult siblings and offspring, which can offer information, practical advice, support, and opportunities for advocacy. If you have denied or minimized your own needs in the past, a support group provides an opportunity for validation. As one family member wrote, "We try to focus on ourselves because we've always been so dominated by the experience of mental illness."

Finally, you may profit from personal counseling or psychotherapy. Counseling sometimes refers to briefer, less intensive, and more supportive forms of treatment. Psychotherapy is appropriate for severe and deep-seated problems. Often, however, the terms are used interchangeably, as we do in *How to Cope with Mental Illness in Your Family*. Family members often tell us they've benefited from professional counseling. Here is one woman's account:

> I survived childhood largely on the belief that if I could hurry and grow up, I could "fix" my mother. I also believed that

adulthood would bring wonderful things for me, since I was having all my hard times as a child. The shattering of these beliefs, which hit me in my thirties, created an extreme crisis for me. In therapy I have resolved my feelings about my mother.

Next we'll tell you more about two important resources: support groups and professional counseling. Our discussion will help you understand these resources and decide whether they might be helpful in your case.

JOINING A SUPPORT GROUP

We've talked about the importance of social support, which generally refers to the role that other people can play in protecting us from the adverse effects of stress. Joining a support group is one way to increase the social support in your life. Sometimes support groups are called self-help or mutual support groups. All of these terms refer to a group of people with a common problem who meet to help themselves and one another.

Support groups for families are now available in most communities, although most of them are designed for parents whose son or daughter has mental illness. Some communities also have specialized groups for adult siblings and offspring. You can locate the nearest group by contacting your local mental health organizations or state NAMI office. Groups can be offered in a variety of professional and community settings, and can be facilitated by family members, by professionals, or by a family-professional team. There are also resources available if you wish to develop a support group yourself. Many local NAMI groups are now offering the Journey of Hope Family Education and Support Program, which provides training in facilitating a support group. A *Group Facilitator's Guide* developed by Rex but now out of print is summarized in Appendix C.

In the following vignette, a facilitator of an actual support-group meeting describes the group for new members:

This is a self-help group for siblings and children of the mentally ill. Each person in this group is required to maintain confidentiality. The group encourages education and self-development. We don't promote any particular view, we give advice only when it is invited, and the advice is given only from our own perspective—what works for me. We encourage openness. Our mission is to recognize and build on the special needs, interests, and contributions of adult siblings and children. We discuss issues that affect us and draw upon one another's strengths.

In light of the adaption process that family members undergo, your group is likely to include members at different stages and with different needs. Thus, it is important to be sensitive to the needs of all your group members. If group size permits, your group can be broken down into smaller units whose members share specific needs and goals. Some members may choose to spend additional time telling their stories in "caring and sharing" sessions; others may prefer to direct energy toward advocacy activities. In addition, a "buddy system" might be set up to offer members additional support outside scheduled group meetings.

Whatever your personal circumstances and the nature of your support group, you're likely to share in the benefits experienced by the following sibling:

> To get more information and support, I joined a support group. It was like waking up from a trance—I was amazed how fast my recovery progressed. I have been in this group for nine years and have witnessed remarkable growth in myself and others. My SAC group has become the family and allies I never had.

OBTAINING PROFESSIONAL COUNSELING

Given the personal anguish and demoralization experienced by family members, you may also benefit from professional counseling for yourself. You may find, for example, that your involvement in a support group has met many of your needs. However, you continue to experience depression in response to your relative's illness and to derive little pleasure from your own life. Counseling may offer you some assistance, as it did for a majority of participants in our survey.

More than three-fourths of these family members had received psychotherapy. Among those who were under age eleven at the onset of their relative's illness or who were both a sibling and a child, 90 percent had undergone personal therapy. Almost all reported that it was beneficial. It is important to note, however, that few of these family members had other services available to them; they may have turned to therapy as the only resort.

Earlier we suggested that you consider professional counseling if you experience any of the following: severe and persistent depression; sharp mood swings; severe anxiety, panic, or fear; abuse of alcohol or drugs; or significant health or physical problems without an underlying cause. In addition, you may also wish to consider professional counseling if you experience:

- an unresolved grieving process that undermines your relationships and satisfactions in the present;

- intense anger that is directed inward or at your other family members;

- persistent and severe distress in response to your relative's symptoms;

- a sense that your own life has been interrupted;

- significant problems related to your personal legacy, such as entrenched feelings of poor self-esteem;

- significant problems related to your occupational legacy, such as a sense of unfulfilled potential;

- significant problems related to your interpersonal legacy, such as difficulty with trust and intimacy; or

- significant problems related to your family legacy, such as conflicts between your personal and family commitments.

Our discussion may help you decide whether you want to pursue professional counseling. We'll talk about potential benefits and risks, explain how to proceed, discuss some approaches to counseling, and tell you how to get the most out of your experience. But first let's hear from two family members who talk about their own experiences in therapy. The first woman recalls her early years with a father who had major depression. She entered her adulthood with little recognition of the legacy of her early years. In fact, she attempted to avoid thinking about her anguished childhood. It was only during therapy that she began to understand the role of her childhood experiences in her marital problems:

> I related to my husband as I had related to my father. I rarely communicated my feelings to him and I felt responsible for his. I pulled away from him when things became difficult and built up a wall that would keep potential pain at bay. Fortunately, recognizing these discoveries, understanding them, and working toward changing them has made the difference in our relationship. Hopefully, it has begun healthier relationship patterns for our children.

Another family member—this time a sibling—also talks about the benefits of professional counseling. She too found that her early experience with mental illness had an adverse impact on her marriage. Her therapist helped her see the connection between her earlier encounter with her sister's schizophrenia and her current difficulties:

> After I began psychotherapy, it didn't take long for my therapist to point out that I had had more than the average life crises and had no reason to feel ashamed of my need for help. My sister's illness had deeply affected me, and I'd never consciously realized it. Once I began to learn about schizophrenia, my life came into better focus, and I felt more in control. This crisis in our life was a new beginning for us. We began to reconstruct our marriage.

Potential Benefits and Risks

There is much evidence for the effectiveness of psychotherapy in assisting a majority of individuals (approximately two-thirds in most studies). As a family member, you may gain:

- insight into the SaC Syndrome and its personal meaning;

- assistance in establishing more constructive relationships;

- more effective methods of coping;

- a reduced level of distress;

- more positive feelings about yourself and your future; and

- support in creating a more fulfilling life.

The following woman grew up with a mother who had schizophrenia. Even decades after her initial encounter with mental illness, she found therapy worthwhile, learning how the illness had profoundly changed her life:

> It wasn't until I sought therapy for anxiety upon my divorce that I began to understand some of the dynamics of my family and myself. I have missed much, have just begun to recognize what has been lost or even never realized. It has taken me a long time to finally face the original problem. Therapy opened doors to my self and answered many puzzling questions.

There are risks associated with any treatment, whether it is medical or psychological. In the case of psychotherapy, these risks are called "negative treatment effects." Negative treatment effects can result from general problems, including deficient training and skill on the part of the therapist, low motivation on the part of the client, or problems in the therapist-client relationship, such as poor communication or absence of rapport. There are also specific risks associated with your role as a family member.

First, it is important not to "overprescribe" therapy for problems that family members can resolve on their own or through a support group. Under these circumstances, intensive therapy may add to your feelings of helplessness and result in a substantial investment of time, energy, and money that cannot be justified. On the other hand, a brief course of supportive counseling may be less demanding and more helpful.

Second, there is the risk of harm if your therapist adheres to older theoretical models that incorporated negative assumptions about families, who were often held accountable for the serious mental illness of their members. Such therapy is likely to increase your feelings of guilt and add significantly to your subjective burden. One sibling highlights these risks:

> I was sixteen when my fourteen-year-old brother had his first psychotic episode. He was hospitalized for most of my adolescence. His illness was the most devastating episode of my entire life. I was ashamed, I was afraid, I was confused. I was involved in family-therapy sessions that put the blame on the family. It was awful.

Third, especially if you were exposed to traumatic events as a young child, you may have buried painful memories and feelings that can resurface in therapy with an intensity that leaves you feeling overwhelmed and immobilized. It is essential for your therapist to provide a controlled confrontation in a safe setting, as memories and feelings are reconnected with the original event. Even with careful attention to the risk of emotional flooding, you may experience considerable distress during therapy. One man conveys the difficulties involved in resolving the traumatic childhood experiences associated with his mother's mental illness: "Right now, what I mostly see is pain all around me. Every time I rub up against reality I feel like crying."

Finally, many therapists do not have expertise concerned with serious mental illness or with the experiences and needs of family members. Thus, there is the risk that you will feel misunderstood by your therapist and will find therapy unproductive. The following multigenerational family member talks about his unsatisfactory experiences in therapy:

> Over the years, I have spent time with several different individual and group therapists. My attempts at therapy have been largely disappointing. Little was done for me. It was frustrating. So much wasted time, money, and energy. This can only add to your despair.

How to Proceed

Once you have decided to seek therapy for yourself, you need to find an appropriate therapist. Several kinds of professionals are likely to offer

outpatient treatment in your community. Psychiatrists have a medical degree (M.D.) and additional training in psychiatry; they are able to pre-
scribe medication. Clinical psychologists have a doctorate (Ph.D. or
Psy.D.) in psychology, with specialized training in assessment and treatment. There are also other professionals who have advanced training in
counseling and psychotherapy, including clinical social workers (M.S.W.
or L.C.S.W.), marriage and family therapists (M.M.F.T.), and various
kinds of counselors (M.A., M.S., or M.Ed.). Often the best referral source
is another family member who has been satisfied with his or her therapist.
Local and state professional associations can also make general referrals.

You may wish to interview two or three therapists before making a
choice. Relevant information includes:

- the background of your therapist;

- the costs involved in therapy, including fees and insurance re-
  imbursement;

- the therapeutic process, including your sessions, contacts outside of regular appointments, and possible risks and benefits;

- the anticipated length of therapy;

- the goals and approach of therapy;

- the behavior expected of you and your therapist;

- consultation with colleagues, such as meetings with a supervi-
  sor;

- office policies, such as those concerned with record keeping,
  access to your files, and canceled appointments;

- any limitations of your confidential relationship with your
  therapist; and

- audio- or videotaping of sessions.

In addition to these general issues, you may want to ask a prospective
therapist about his or her knowledge of serious mental illness, about prior
experience working with family members, and about what is expected to
be most helpful for you. Because relatively few therapists have expertise

concerned with the experiences and needs of siblings and offspring, you may wish to suggest some reading material, including this book, once you find an appropriate therapist.

Finally, your emotional response is very important. Therapy involves more than a dispassionate recount of your life events. You need to feel understood even during the initial session. Empathy, warmth, and sensitivity are cornerstones in your healing. The first clinician you talk with may not be the one you choose as your therapist.

Before beginning therapy, you should have some idea of your goals in therapy, which can be very broad if you are experiencing significant problems in many areas of your life or relatively narrow if you are dealing with a specific situation or concern. A number of general treatment goals are appropriate for family members under these circumstances. For example, you can benefit from information and support, from improved coping skills, from an opportunity to reframe your personal and familial experience in more constructive ways, and from expression and resolution of your emotional burden.

Approaches to Counseling

Once you have chosen to undertake professional counseling, you need to know something about therapeutic format and about the strategies and techniques used by your therapist.

FORMAT. The format you select determines the number of individuals who will be present and the nature of the interpersonal context. Alternative formats include the following:

- individual therapy;

- marital or couple therapy;

- family therapy, which may include all members of the immediate or extended family; and

- group therapy, which may focus on a common issue or include members with different concerns.

Given the diversity among family members, each of these formats has potential value and each carries possible risks. Many family members who responded to our survey had benefited from individual psychotherapy. In your case, individual therapy may be helpful if you desire the privacy and intimacy of a confidential relationship, are experiencing inner conflict, or are having difficulty resolving your emotional burden. One family member wrote of his experience in therapy: "I wanted to give the scared little boy inside me every opportunity to mourn." Individual therapy also carries some risks, including the risk that your legacy will be defined a personal mental health problem instead of a universal experience shared by other siblings and offspring.

If you are experiencing significant problems in your close relationships, couple or family therapy may be helpful. For example, family therapy may be indicated if your family has difficulty communicating or is unable to cope adequately with the mental illness. At the same time, family therapy results in loss of privacy, may increase your family disruption, and may fail to address your individual problems and concerns.

In our research, for instance, several family members mentioned negative experiences in family therapy, including the frustration of attending family sessions when their relative was exhibiting psychotic symptoms. One sibling wrote: "Every time we tried to get some direction on how to deal with this as a unit, my sister would stand up, threatening violence at times. There wasn't much good that came out of that experience."

Group therapy is a relatively economical format that is similar in many respects to a support group. This format is likely to reduce your feelings of isolation, although there is the risk that your individual issues and concerns will receive insufficient attention.

STRATEGIES AND TECHNIQUES. In addition to format, you should also be familiar with therapeutic strategies and techniques, which are the technical interventions used by your therapist to produce change. The orientations (or "schools") of therapists often influence their approach to therapy. Some important approaches include:

- psychodynamic and psychoanalytic therapy, which emphasize the role of early childhood experience and inner conflict, and often involve analysis of dreams, of free association (expression of thoughts without reservation), and of the therapeutic relationship;

- cognitive-behavioral therapy, which emphasizes present thoughts and behaviors, and the strategies that can modify maladaptive patterns of thinking and behaving;

- client-centered therapy, which emphasizes support and validation (for example, through unconditional positive regard), as well as the innate potential of human beings for self-actualization;

- existential therapy, which emphasizes questions of meaning and value, and the importance of choice and personal responsibility;

- expressive therapy, which makes use of painting, music, dance, and writing;

- gestalt therapy, which emphasizes present circumstances, the use of role playing, and a holistic conception of personality that strives to integrate mind, emotions, and body; and

- interpersonal therapy, which focuses on past and present relationships.

In addition, many therapists also practice variations or combinations of the above.

As a family member, you may benefit from many of these approaches, which may offer an opportunity to explore your early childhood, to change maladaptive patterns of thinking and behavior, to receive support and validation, to understand the personal meaning of the mental illness, to channel your feelings through expressive therapy, and to examine your experiences and relationships. Given the far-reaching impact of the SaC Syndrome, you may prefer to work with an eclectic therapist who selects strategies and techniques based on what is most likely to be helpful for you rather than on a particular school.

Depending on your needs, goals, and resources, you may decide on a brief course of supportive counseling, which is appropriate if you have functioned reasonably well in the past or there is significant current stress in your life (therapy takes time, energy, and money). In contrast, you may benefit from long-term psychotherapy if you have serious mental health problems yourself or are experiencing severe problems in several areas of your life. One sibling told us: "Seven years of psychotherapy has helped me to value my own needs." This woman also feels she has benefited considerably from long-term therapy:

> I sank into an eight-year depression. My mother's illness completely interrupted my life. Her illness progressed, and I found myself isolated and powerless in dealing with it. The establishment repeatedly told me that there was nothing they could do unless my mother wished help. My mother would not agree to see a doctor. I've been in therapy for eleven years now. That's the only good result I can see coming out of this tragedy.

What is most important, ultimately, is whether you feel that the therapy provides you with a valuable experience.

How to Get the Most Out of Therapy

If professional counseling is part of your journey of hope and healing, you'll find your relationship with your therapist is the most important ingredient. This relationship is sometimes described as a therapeutic or working alliance. Often, a trusting relationship develops within the first few sessions, as you begin to feel understood and valued by your therapist. Many factors can affect your therapeutic alliance. For example, your personal qualities are important, including:

- your motivation for therapy;
- your attitude toward yourself, your therapist, and your therapy;
- your self-understanding, personality traits, and coping styles;
- your openness and honesty about yourself and your family; and
- your patience in exploring your early years and in resolving deep-seated problems.

The following qualities of your therapist are also important:

- competence, warmth, empathy, genuineness, and caring;

- knowledge of serious mental illness;

- familiarity with the experiences and needs of families;

- sensitivity to your special issues and concerns as a sibling or offspring of someone with mental illness; and

- willingness to acknowledge the strengths and resources of family members and to avoid pathologizing them.

Finally, a number of interactional factors are likely to promote the development of a constructive therapeutic alliance:

- similarities between you and your therapist, including similar interests, values, and beliefs; and

- the commitment, involvement, and positive expectations shared by you and your therapist.

As the following multigenerational family member affirms, therapy offers many potential benefits:

> I did not explore therapy until age thirty-five. Professionals can be a wonderful vehicle to bring out repressed pain and guilt. It's hard to move forward without opening up blocked tears. Once I allowed myself to really cry, I unburdened more than I ever thought I could carry. Besides making me feel relieved, I felt human—a healthy human for the first time.

MILEPOSTS

During this leg of your journey, you've continued to name and tame your SaC Syndrome, now focusing largely on the taming process. Mileposts of this leg include:

- understanding of your adaptation process;

- awareness of your needs as a family member; and

- familiarity with the resources that can facilitate your adaptation process and address your needs.

As you continue to confront and resolve your personal legacy, your anguish will gradually diminish. Each time you tell your story to your support group or your therapist—the naming and taming process—it will lose some of its power. Ultimately, the mental illness will become merely one event in your life; the painful territory will begin to shrink. At the same time, this process is never entirely finished, but continues to unfold throughout your life.

There are two legs yet to follow on your journey of hope and healing. The next leg involves revising your legacy and translating your insights into action.

Chapter 6

REVISING
YOUR LEGACY

❧

I was so depressed and lonely. I even thought of suicide. For many years, I looked for answers for my brother's problems, never realizing I had to find myself first. I had to leave home to survive. I have—being in therapy, learning I'm okay. I'm now married and successful in my job as an elementary guidance counselor. I am what I wanted to be—a caring, nurturing person.

THESE ARE THE WORDS of a resilient family member—someone who managed to triumph over the adversity in her life and to fulfill her own hopes and dreams. In the earlier legs of your journey, you gained new insights into the SaC Syndrome and its meaning for your life. During this leg, you'll learn how to translate these insights into action and to forge a resilient path yourself.

Although you can't change your past or your family circumstances, you can alter your view of these events, as well as their impact on your present thoughts, feelings, and behavior. You can also develop a Personal Action Plan that can guide you in making beneficial changes in your life. Whatever the challenges of the past, in the present you have an opportunity to renew your relationships, to make new choices, and to pursue new goals.

As you gradually revise your legacy as a family member, you'll begin to mitigate your painful memories and to recapture your energy for your present and your future. No longer the major force, the mental illness will be placed in perspective, as a single event in your life.

LANDMARKS

There are three major landmarks on the fifth leg of your journey. First, as you prepare to transform your new understanding into reality, you need to enhance your coping effectiveness. You'll learn about the resources that can assist you.

Second, we'll help you develop a Personal Action Plan to guide you toward a more satisfying and productive future. We've talked about the importance of accepting what you can't change. It's just as important to acknowledge what you *can* change and to focus your energy where it can do the most good.

Third, you'll learn how to deal with the mental health system. Perhaps you've already encountered the system as your relative's advocate. If so, you may have found the system unresponsive to your family's needs. Indeed, the system can sometimes seem like a formidable and recalcitrant foe. We'll help you learn how to turn it into an ally—in the present or in the future.

After you've passed these landmarks, you'll find you've embarked on a resilient path yourself.

ENHANCING YOUR COPING EFFECTIVENESS

In many ways, your journey of hope and healing is about change—and change requires courage. You've needed courage to confront your painful past and to name and tame your SaC Syndrome. You also need courage to recognize and discard the maladaptive patterns of the past.

Our old patterns—however unproductive they may be—are comfortable and familiar. Moving in new directions can be unsettling. For example, if you learned as a child to avoid painful emotions by denying or ignoring them, you may worry you'll be engulfed if you finally allow your feelings to surface. If you dealt with conflict by denying your own needs, your present efforts to stand up for your rights may by accompanied by considerable uneasiness. If you avoided others to protect yourself from further pain or rejection, your attempts to reach out may be coupled with substantial apprehension.

Thus, you need courage to deal with the anxiety that always accompanies change. You also need courage to deal with the inevitable uncertainty. Even when we have a clear sense of where we want to go—a difficult enough task itself—and have prepared for change, there is no guarantee that we'll be successful. But we can increase the likelihood of success by enhancing our coping effectiveness.

Understanding Your Coping Resources

Coping resources are those elements in your life that can offer assistance under conditions of severe stress. As we discussed earlier, there are many personal, family, and social factors that can affect your ability to cope with your family circumstances. In our own research, we explored the coping resources of adult siblings and offspring. We asked them to rate the relative value of various resources during childhood, adolescence, and adulthood. These resources included:

- their personal qualities;

- their family;

- their friends;

- an advocacy organization, such as NAMI;

- a support group;

- mental health professionals; and

- clergy.

Many participants emphasized the value of NAMI, the family advocacy organization. One multigenerational family member wrote about her "invaluable" experiences in NAMI, citing "the knowledge I gained, the friendships I developed, the feelings I began to recognize and deal with because of this association with others who were going through similar experiences." Similarly, participants frequently mentioned the benefits of a specialized support group for adult siblings and offspring:

With the nurturance of the group, the healing for me has come through the opportunity to express negative feelings, to share grief over our many losses, and to learn about self-care and setting limits. Besides the tears and anger, we are healing each other with laughter and fun as well.

When we examined the overall availability of resources during the three developmental phases, we found that children had the fewest resources available to them. Thus, during their period of greatest need, young family members have limited resources to assist them in coping with this cataclysmic event. As one family member said, "I don't think *anything* has helped."

Aside from their personal qualities as adolescents, it was not until adulthood that these family members found the full range of coping resources helpful. In addition to our list, some respondents cited other useful resources:

- educational materials;
- creative activity;
- regular exercise;
- volunteer work; and
- spirituality.

A number of family members emphasized the importance of spirituality in their lives. A man who has two siblings with mental illness sought peace and guidance through his belief in a higher power: "My spirituality has helped me to accept my family members' illnesses, to become more resilient, and to set limits within my life." An adult offspring agreed:

Faith can be strengthened by hardship. I perceived my religious faith as a form of "basic training." Living with the mentally ill is living in a war zone—a psychological rather than a physical war. If I must enter a battleground, I would rather enter with basic training than without it.

Reinforcing Your Personal Resources

Our survey participants told us their personal qualities were their most important resource—at every stage of development. There are many ways you can strengthen your own abilities. For example, as we discussed earlier, you can develop essential coping skills, including effective communication, problem-solving, conflict-management, assertiveness, symptom-management, and stress-management skills.

You can also try to develop a healthy appraisal of the mental illness. Appraisal refers to the way you evaluate the nature and importance of the illness. Earlier we talked about your family's appraisal—the family meaning of the illness. A positive family appraisal might include a hopeful attitude toward your relative's prospects for recovery and a belief that your family has the resources to cope with the challenges accompanying mental illness.

Your personal appraisal is also important in determining the way you feel about your family situation and even how well you are able to cope with it. A cornerstone of your adaptation process is your ability to restore a sense of meaning and coherence to your life. Mental illness looms as an ominous—even uncontrollable—event in most families. As you struggle to find meaning in this event, you'll gradually recover a sense of order, purpose, and control in your life.

In *Composing a Life,* Mary Catherine Bateson talks about the human search for meaning, noting that we give meaning to the present through a continual process of reinterpreting the past and reimagining the future. We are, in her view, all storytellers. Listen as the following family member tells her story:

> It's made me a much stronger person. It's actually made me happier in that I appreciate life and all I have to enjoy. I never get depressed, because I remind myself how lucky I am to have my mental health. I never complain or let life's little irritations get to me. My sister's illness has made me patient and understanding of people with any type of handicap.

Building on your enhanced coping effectiveness, a Personal Action Plan can help you make desirable changes in your life.

DEVELOPING A PERSONAL ACTION PLAN

Now that you've come to terms with your past and its impact on your present life, you're ready to decide upon an action plan and to implement your plan. We'll offer some suggestions for drafting a Personal Action Plan that can guide your progress. The plan includes eight components: taking care of yourself, taking charge of your life, accepting what you cannot change, maintaining a hopeful attitude, cultivating your personal garden, learning about mental illness, improving your coping skills, and strengthening your personal support network.

Taking Care of Yourself

1. PRACTICE GOOD SELF-CARE. If you're like many siblings and offspring you may be so involved in meeting the needs of others that you sometimes forget to take care of yourself. Develop healthy habits for daily living that meet your needs for sleep, nutrition, exercise, and relaxation. Also do something special for yourself on a regular basis.

2. STRIVE TO MAINTAIN A NORMAL LIFESTYLE. Expand activities and relationships outside your family. Aim for reasonable stability and a comfortable rhythm of daily life. Avoid assuming a crisis mode that keeps you anticipating the next emergency even when things are calm.

3. MAINTAIN A SATISFACTORY BALANCE IN YOUR LIFE. Find ways to fulfill your commitments to others without neglecting your own needs. Remember that caregiving is only one of your roles; don't let it define your relationships.

4. ENHANCE YOUR ABILITY TO LOVE, TO WORK, AND TO PLAY. Seek out people who value and care for you. Find meaningful work that showcases your talents. Take time to unwind in pleasurable activities; build in brief getaways.

5. MOURN YOUR LOSSES. Grieving is a necessary, normal, and natural process. Acknowledge your losses, give yourself time and space to mourn, and then move on.

6. SEEK PROFESSIONAL COUNSELING IF APPROPRIATE. If you remain consumed by your family circumstances and unable to derive much pleasure from your own life, consider counseling an investment in your future.

Taking Charge of Your Life

1. PLACE THE MENTAL ILLNESS IN PERSPECTIVE, AS A SINGLE EVENT IN YOUR LIFE. Apply a wide-angle lens that captures your other experiences, relationships, and opportunities, and your future as well as your past.

2. SEPARATE YOURSELF FROM THE MENTAL ILLNESS IN YOUR FAMILY. Also separate your family from the illness, which is only one family event, and your relative from the illness, never losing sight of the human being behind the symptoms.

3. LEARN FROM THE PAST. Free yourself from earlier maladaptive patterns and choices. Every day offers the opportunity to make new choices and to pursue new goals.

4. ACCEPT AND APPRECIATE YOURSELF. Be honest with yourself, set realistic goals, and acknowledge your limits. Accept your best as good enough; don't aim for perfection. For yourself and others, focus on strengths rather than shortcomings.

5. BE WILLING TO TAKE RISKS. Changing familiar patterns can be frightening. Decide upon a course of change, prepare yourself for action, and gradually translate your plan into reality.

6. LEARN TO SET LIMITS. Don't let the mental illness of your relative take over your life. You can live only one life—make sure it is the one you choose.

Accepting What You Cannot Change

1. ACCEPT YOUR FAMILY CIRCUMSTANCES. The mental illness is etched on your family slate, leaving an indelible mark on all your lives. You cannot alter that reality.

2. ACCEPT THE PAIN IN YOUR FAMILY. Your family has suffered irrevocable losses. You cannot change that fact or compensate them for their suffering.

3. ACCEPT YOUR RELATIVE'S MENTAL ILLNESS. Your relative has also suffered major losses. You cannot make your relative well.

4. ACCEPT YOUR OWN SORROW. You too have experienced significant losses in the past. Acknowledge and grieve your losses; they are woven into the fabric of your life.

5. ACCEPT THE LEGACY FOR YOUR PRESENT LIFE. You carry the weight of your family experience, which is likely to influence your thoughts, feelings, and behavior.

6. ACCEPT THE MEANING OF MENTAL ILLNESS FOR YOUR FUTURE. The illness has not only affected your past and your present. It also colors your future, leaving a residue of uncertainty for your relative, your family, and yourself.

Maintaining a Hopeful Attitude

1. STRIVE FOR A POSITIVE ATTITUDE. Reframe to emphasize strengths as well as limitations, gains as well as losses, and hope as well as despair. Preserve your sense of humor.

2. REVISE YOUR FAMILY EXPERIENCE OF MENTAL ILLNESS. Along with their experience of mental illness, your family shares an intricate tapestry woven of common bonds, memories, rituals, celebrations, losses, and myths.

3. RECONSIDER YOUR RELATIVE'S EXPERIENCE OF MENTAL ILLNESS. Along with the limitations that result from the illness, your relative has the potential for recovery and for an improved quality of life.

4. REVIEW YOUR PAST. Along with your anguish, your experience with mental illness may have given you increased understanding, more tolerance and compassion, and greater appreciation of life's treasures.

5. INVEST IN YOUR PRESENT. Whatever your past experiences, you have an opportunity in the present to gain insight, to achieve resolution, to reclaim your territory, and to reallocate your energy.

6. PLAN FOR YOUR FUTURE. Whatever your past choices, you have an opportunity in the future to make new choices, to pursue new goals, to rebuild current relationships, and to form new ones.

Cultivating Your Personal Garden

1. NOURISH YOUR TALENTS. Promote your talents as a writer, artist, actor, dancer, or musician. Develop new talents.

2. EXPLORE YOUR INTERESTS. Expand your interests in gardening, hiking, camping, crafts, or exercise. Develop new interests.

3. RECONSIDER YOUR OCCUPATION. People typically make four major career changes in their lives, including time spent at home. Consider changing your career or pursuing education or training that can unlock new opportunities.

4. EXPAND YOUR EMOTIONAL AND INTELLECTUAL HORIZONS. Seek out new people, experiences, and activities.

5. ENLARGE YOUR GEOGRAPHICAL BOUNDARIES. Travel by land, sea, and air. Visit new terrains, regions, and countries.

6. HEAR THE CALL TO SERVICE. Contribute your gifts to others. Volunteer your energy to a valued cause or group.

Learning About Mental Illness

1. LEARN ABOUT MENTAL ILLNESS AND ITS TREATMENT. Many resources are available (see Appendix A).

2. LEARN ABOUT THE MENTAL HEALTH SYSTEM AND COMMUNITY RESOURCES. Contact professionals or a local family support group.

3. LEARN ABOUT THE FAMILY EXPERIENCE OF MENTAL ILLNESS AND ABOUT THE EXPERIENCES OF INDIVIDUAL FAMILY MEMBERS. Read the personal accounts of parents, spouses, and people with mental illness themselves.

4. LEARN ABOUT THE SPECIAL IMPACT ON SIBLINGS AND OFFSPRING. For example, read the personal accounts of family members, such as *Anguished Voices* (see Appendix A).

5. LEARN ABOUT YOUR RELATIVE'S EXPERIENCE OF MENTAL ILLNESS. Connect with the person behind the illness. Ask about his or her symptoms, struggle, coping strategies, and hopes for the future.

6. LEARN ABOUT THE EXPERIENCES OF THE REST OF YOUR FAMILY. Ask them about their experiences, concerns, and needs. Share feelings and coping strategies.

Improving Your Coping Skills

1. BE PREPARED. Anticipate your challenges, develop the essential skills and strategies, marshal your allies, and take action when necessary.

2. AVOID INEFFECTIVE COPING STRATEGIES. Each of the following offers short-term gains: denial, withdrawal, alcohol and drugs, and negative emotions, such as anger and resentment. However, these strategies all undermine your coping efforts in the long term.

3. IMPROVE YOUR COMMUNICATION SKILLS. Effective listening is active, nonjudgmental, responsive, and empathic. Effective expression is clear, complete, direct, and supportive.

4. REFINE YOUR PROBLEM-SOLVING AND CONFLICT-MANAGEMENT SKILLS. Aim for a win-win solution that respects the interests of all parties and results in a mutually acceptable option. Create an atmosphere of mutual tolerance and respect.

5. DEVELOP YOUR STRESS-MANAGEMENT SKILLS. Understand the nature of stress, as well as the kinds and sources of stress in

your life. When possible, avoid stressful situations or reduce the level of stress. When stress is inevitable, learn to manage it more effectively.

6. ENHANCE YOUR ASSERTIVENESS SKILLS. Learn to stand up for your legitimate rights, to refuse to let others take advantage of you, and to meet your own needs without violating the rights of others. Speak up and let others know how you feel.

Strengthening Your Personal Support Network

1. BUILD LIFELINES TO OTHER PEOPLE. They are your most important resource. Share your story with them and listen to theirs.

2. CHERISH YOUR PRESENT RELATIONSHIPS WITH YOUR FAMILY, PARTNER, FRIENDS, AND COLLEAGUES. Develop new relationships that can nurture and console you.

3. SEEK OUT OTHERS WHO HAVE UNDERGONE THE FAMILY EXPERIENCE OF MENTAL ILLNESS. They can validate your experience, share your anguish, and offer practical advice.

4. CONTACT PROFESSIONALS AND OTHER SERVICE PROVIDERS. They can inform you about mental illness, the service delivery system, and community resources.

5. JOIN A SUPPORT GROUP FOR ADULT SIBLINGS AND OFFSPRING. Organize a group if none is available in your community (see Appendix C).

6. BECOME ACTIVE IN AN ADVOCACY GROUP. Family advocacy organizations, such as NAMI, have already had a significant impact at state and national levels. As an advocate on the local level, you can improve the lives of people with mental illness in your community.

DEALING WITH THE MENTAL HEALTH SYSTEM

For most of *How to Cope with Mental Illness in Your Family,* we've focused on your personal experiences, needs, and concerns. So you may be surprised to find a section on the mental health system. But in fact the system is an important part of your personal journey. In our work we've heard repeatedly from family members about their frustration with a system that often fails to meet the needs of their relative or their family. As one sibling lamented, "In twenty-five years, no case manager, community support worker, or therapist has ever taken the time to call me or my sister about anything—it's as if we didn't exist." Another family member complained that "the gauntlet of mental health professionals all claim authority, but none will accept responsibility."

In this section, we'll give you some essential information about the mental health system, explaining why the system is important to family members, providing a brief historical overview, exploring relationships between families and professionals, and discussing your personal involvement with the system. Even if your own encounters with the system have been limited in the past, the future may bring you into greater contact. As we mentioned earlier, almost all of our survey participants expressed concern about present or future caregiving for their relative.

Why the System Is Important

The mental health system is important for your relative, for your family as a unit, and for you personally. For example, the system is essential for the treatment, rehabilitation, and recovery of your relative, who may benefit from a wide range of services. These include mental health, physical health, social, rehabilitative, vocational, and residential services. The manner in which these services are delivered is also important. Many people with mental illness do not receive regular services, perhaps due to a lack of transportation or even to the symptoms of mental illness, which may prevent them from understanding their need for treatment. Thus, services should be delivered in an assertive, individualized, coordinated, and continuous manner.

They should also be delivered out in the community—wherever people with mental illness reside. Remember, approximately one-third of the homeless are people with mental illness. Indeed, the threat of homelessness haunts many family members: "I'm doing everything I can to find some way to care for my brother and my dad, so they don't wind up on the street. That's my biggest fear." Sometimes this threat becomes a grim reality. A sibling described his brother's eviction from his residence following their mother's death: "After twenty-three years of being sheltered, he left with only a shopping bag of belongings. He was now homeless."

The availability of a truly comprehensive and humane system of care would transform the lives of families, who often pay a high price for the gaps in the current system. This family member portrays her feelings of helplessness in the face of an insensitive and unresponsive system:

> My mother started getting worse. She wasn't hurting anyone, she wasn't violent. She was just causing pain to five small children. That didn't seem to really matter. We twice went to court and weren't able to have her committed. Eventually my mother was roaming the streets and was picked up by the police.

Fortunately, we also hear from family members whose experiences with the system have been more positive. One sibling talked about the many factors that had promoted positive changes in her sister, including supportive, caring, knowledgeable, and understanding staff, as well as an effective program designed to maximize the potential of each individual. She wrote: "The growth I have seen in my sister is indeed heart-warming."

In addition to services for your relative, the mental health system is important for your family. As we've discussed, your family has compelling needs for information about mental illness and community resources, for skills to cope with the illness, and for support. Particularly at the time of the initial diagnosis or during periods of inpatient treatment for your relative, the system can meet these needs and serve as an essential resource for your family. As a sibling relates, this potential is not always fulfilled. Following the death of his mother (his brother's caregiver), he flew in to talk with the professionals who were treating his brother. But "the psychiatrist gave me nothing specific about his findings and only vaguely shared that my brother was 'angry at the world.'" It was only later that he discovered his brother's correct diagnosis—schizophrenia.

When the mental health system fails to address the needs of families, there are often devastating consequences for young family members. A sibling said that her parents received little support from professionals and died without coming to terms with the mental illness of their daughter. She grew up feeling responsible for making everyone happy and for meeting their needs ahead of her own. In response to one of our questions, she said, "I did not let my light shine, because how could I have a great life when those in my family were so miserable?" Clearly, if her family's needs had been met when she was growing up, her own journey would have been less troubled and her burden less weighty.

In addition to the needs of your family as a unit, you also have special needs as a sibling or offspring of someone with mental illness. Regrettably, your needs have rarely been addressed—or even acknowledged—by the system. In the words of one sibling, "As a child I needed concrete explanations of what was going on. Siblings need help with their fear of becoming mentally ill themselves, help sorting out ordinary adolescent reactions, and help in their relationship with their brother or sister." Yet too often their needs remain unheeded. As one family member asserted, "Professionals need to prevent the painful consequences that often don't show up for years."

To assist you in understanding the system and making it more responsive to your family's needs, we'll provide a brief overview of the historical context and of family-professional relationships.

The Historical Context

Throughout human history, people with disabilities, including those with mental illness, have been subject to discrimination, neglect, ridicule, and devaluation. Prior to World War II, the treatment of choice was segregation, and many people with mental illness spent their adult lives in state mental hospitals, sequestered from their families and their communities. In spite of their limitations, institutional settings did offer a sanctuary for vulnerable individuals who were often unwelcome and misunderstood in the larger society. From the perspective of modern history, this was the era of institutionalization and segregation.

During the postwar period, several powerful forces challenged the philosophies and policies of the institutional era and ultimately culminated in deinstitutionalization. These forces included the following:

- the community mental health movement, with its emphasis on the debilitating and dehumanizing effects of large hospitals, and the beneficial effects of treating individuals close to their families, homes, and jobs;

- economic influences, including the belief that it was less expensive to provide community-based treatment;

- advances in psychopharmacology that resulted in control of the most disabling and disruptive symptoms for many individuals;

- various forms of psychosocial treatment that were developed to meet the needs of this population; and

- the civil rights movement, which ushered in an era of concern for individual liberties, including those of people confined in mental hospitals.

As President John F. Kennedy declared in his message to Congress on February 5, 1963, there was to be a "bold new approach" to the treatment of people with serious mental illness. This second era of deinstitutionalization lasted until approximately the mid-1980s. The goals of deinstitutionalization were to transfer the residents of state hospitals to community-based programs and to prevent the institutionalization of new residents through early treatment. In fact, the state hospital census has declined from a peak of 560,000 residents in 1955 to fewer than 90,000 by the mid-1990s. But in many respects, the initial promise of deinstitutionalization was not fully realized.

Problems characterizing this second era include the following:

- absence of treatment for many people with serious mental illness;

- their movement into the correctional system and the ranks of the homeless;

- failure to allocate sufficient resources for community-based care;

- pervasively negative attitudes and low priorities associated with serious mental illness;

- absence of a full range of community-based services; and

- fragmentation of existing services.

These shortcomings continue to characterize the present era, with disastrous consequences for people with mental illness and for their families. Furthermore, even in the contemporary era, family members sometimes encounter the earlier institutions that continue to serve as a last resort for their relatives. The following woman has three family members with mental illness. Over the years, her brother and sister have both spent time in institutions. She recalls visiting her sister in a state hospital:

> Thinking about visiting my sister in the state institution still brings back feelings of horror. It was distressingly like the hospital in *One Flew Over the Cuckoo's Nest*. My sister had been taken there the night before, hauled off by the police. The place was huge, shabby, crowded, frightening—not a place to get well in.

Following the eras of institutional care and deinstitutionalization, we have now embarked on a third era of full community participation and integration. Our present objective is to build a community that meets all the needs of people with mental illness, that respects their rights and dignity, that affirms their potential for growth and recovery, and that maximizes opportunities for them to contribute their talents and gifts. To accomplish this objective, we must develop a comprehensive system of care that can empower people with mental illness to lead meaningful lives in their communities.

As we await the full realization of a truly comprehensive and humane system of care, family members continue to share the frustrations of their relatives. In the words of one woman, "The entire mental health system sorely needs to be revamped. Mental health care should be of the same quality and be given the same respect as the rest of health care services."

Family-Professional Relationships

Family members have been significantly affected by their relationships with professionals in each of these historical eras. For example, during the institutional era families were largely irrelevant to the treatment of their relatives, who often spent their adulthood isolated from the larger society. Little contact occurred—or was needed—between professionals and families.

This isolation changed with deinstitutionalization, which resulted in the discharge of people with mental illness not only to their communities but also to their families. What emerged was a system of care that is as much family-based as community-based. Yet in spite of their essential role, family members often complain that they receive little attention from professionals and other service providers. One man wrote: "My sisters and I have been dealing with our mother's mental illness for over twenty-five years. Nearly twenty years passed before any professional talked to family members like human beings." A sibling echoes his frustration:

> From the beginning I needed more education from professionals, practical tips on how to handle day-to-day situations and the mental health system. I had no sense of what schizophrenia meant. You don't get professional help and support. You're not given any guidance. You are left floundering. So much more can be done for families.

An additional problem is the persistence of earlier theories that assumed serious mental illness resulted from a dysfunctional or pathogenic family environment. Therapies derived from these theories often mandated the treatment of the entire family to identify the causative elements and eliminate them. As a result, family members occasionally found themselves catapulted into family therapy, sometimes without their consent, that met few of their own needs.

Such mandated therapy is in conflict with the professional ethical principle of informed consent. You should be aware that you have a right to make an informed choice about your involvement in therapy. Reflecting on her own experiences in therapy, the following multigenerational family member wrote: "Family therapy is fine, but I think you should have a choice. We all have rights and needs and feelings."

The earlier models that held families accountable for the mental illness resulted in many adverse consequences for families and for family-professional relationships. Some of these include:

- intensifying the feelings of guilt and responsibility experienced by family members;

- alienating families from the mental health system, which was sometimes perceived as insensitive to their anguish and unresponsive to their needs;

- estranging people with mental illness from their families in the climate of blame resulting from professional assumptions of family accountability;

- weakening the support system provided by the family, with an increased risk of relapse or homelessness; and

- undermining the treatment plan, which often requires the collaboration of people with mental illness, their families, and providers of services.

Family members are sensitive to negative assumptions about families on the part of professionals. Struggling to come to terms with his father's suicide and his sister's mental illness, this family member found that his experiences with professionals added to his burden:

> Professionals seem to view siblings through the filters of their statistics and theories rather than listening and trying to understand the complexities of my relationship with my sister. Professionals did not communicate effectively with the family, and my opinions were ignored. While they seemed sympathetic at first to our stressed-out family, they seemed to blame my family for being "dysfunctional."

Fortunately, in the current era we have witnessed many constructive developments in relationships between families and professionals. A number of factors have influenced these developments, including new evidence that serious mental illness is a brain disorder, documentation of the devastating impact of mental illness on families, increasing recognition of their legitimate concerns, and greater recognition of their positive contributions.

In contrast to their earlier unsatisfactory and sometimes adversarial relationships, today families and professionals are more likely to establish collaborative partnerships. These partnerships build on the strengths and expertise of all parties, respect the needs and rights of families, enable families to play an active role in decisions that affect them, and establish mutual goals for treatment and rehabilitation. Many professionals now think in terms of an institutional alliance with families that is designed to meet the needs of all family members, and that complements the therapeutic alliance formed with their relative for purposes of treatment. Both alliances are essential elements of competent professional practice.

Until recently, these collaborative partnerships were largely restricted to parents, who have often served as effective advocates for their adult sons or daughters with serious mental illness. Unfortunately, siblings and offspring have received far less attention from professionals, especially as young family members. In fact, 80 percent of our survey participants said that professionals offered little assistance during their early years. These family members are now finding their rightful place in the family picture as effective advocates for themselves and for their relatives.

The following family member offers some suggestions for professionals:

> Be kind and considerate—have time for them! Encourage them to open up and be accepting of their feelings. Facilitate finding a support group. Don't stigmatize or label. Don't look at them or treat them like they're ill also. Listen to them. Involve them. Treat them with dignity. Help them learn to be assertive, to accept their new problems, and to solve the many problems they face. Support their self-image, plans, and dreams.

Your Involvement with the System

As you were growing up, your family would have benefited from a collaborative model of service delivery that involved your parents as full members of the treatment team. As an adult, you, too, may wish to play a meaningful role in the treatment and rehabilitation of your relative. Indeed, such involvement is essential if you serve as a primary caregiver or informal case manager for your relative. As one family member wrote, "Consider siblings and adult offspring as part of the treatment team because most of us will eventually be primary caregivers."

Even if you do not serve as a caregiver, you may still wish to be kept informed by professionals regarding your relative's progress and to be consulted in matters that affect your family. Or you may may prefer less involvement, perhaps because of geographic distance or other commitments. Even if you're not actively involved in your relative's care in the present, your role could change in the future, possibly when your aging parent can no longer fulfill his or her caregiving function.

Whatever your specific circumstances and wishes, you will benefit from a service delivery system that acknowledges the needs of all members of your family. One barrier to family-professional collaboration often cited by family members is the professional ethical principle of confidentiality. In the words of one family member, "A major problem in the mental health system is the exclusion of relatives under the guise of client confidentiality." Let's take a closer look.

Confidentiality

The ethical principle of confidentiality protects the right of people receiving services from mental health professionals to a confidential therapeutic relationship. There are a few exceptions, including the risk of imminent harm. Problems may arise when the family is a central resource for their relative, when the mental illness has significant consequences for the family, or when decisions regarding treatment and aftercare affect the family. Families should not be expected to assume responsibility for caregiving or case management in the absence of meaningful involvement in treatment. Nor should they have to fight for information from professionals:

> We had to get power of attorney to make the doctor talk to us. We were the ones at home, watching the ill person. We were the ones who knew the behavior firsthand. Blow up that rule that says "right of patient privacy." It should be "right of the whole family." Families are trying desperately to get information or want to communicate because they're worried about their relative.

Under these circumstances, it is a matter of balancing the competing rights of all members of the family. Many family needs can be met by providing relevant but nonconfidential information regarding mental illness, treatment, medication, and symptom management. Actually, much useful information on these matters is available in articles, books, and videotapes for the general public. There are also some strategies for dealing with confidential information. For example, individual professionals can often resolve potential conflicts by negotiating the boundaries of confidentiality to meet the needs of particular families.

In institutional settings conflicts can be resolved by assigning separate staff to serve as family advocates or by including family members on the treatment team. In all settings a release-of-information form can be used to meet the needs of people with mental illness, their family members, and professionals. In any case, a rigid application of the principle of confidentiality is rarely in the best interest of anyone:

> Professionals must reexamine the issue of confidentiality. Our current laws actually thwart continuity of care by excluding family members. I can't understand how this legal assurance of confidentiality and privacy has really helped my brother. In maintaining his confidentiality, professionals have placed my brother and our family in some very dangerous (possibly life-threatening) situations because of a lack of communication.

Although this collaborative approach to treatment often meets the needs of both clients and families, it is important to understand that sometimes clients are unwilling to allow their therapist to talk to family members. For example, clients may worry about family recriminations that focus on their mental illness, may be struggling to achieve more independence from their family, may wish to protect their privacy, or may be overwhelmed by intense feelings of guilt, fear, or shame. As one therapist pointed out, even when professionals would like to have more contact with families, they must sometimes grapple with the reluctance of their client.

FORGING A RESILIENT PATH

We wrote earlier about your capacity for a resilient response to your catastrophic family event. As we've mentioned, in our research we've heard from many family members who said their encounter with mental illness has made them better and stronger people. They've described greater empathy and compassion, more tolerance and understanding, healthier attitudes and priorities, and greater appreciation of life.

A major purpose of *How to Cope with Mental Illness in Your Family* is to help you to maximize your potential for resilience. Some of the best advice comes from other family members:

> Learn whatever you can about the illness. Talk to others about what you are feeling. Don't be ashamed. Learn to help the relative as much as possible without giving up your needs. Become active in teaching the world about mental illness and how terrible it is.

We offer some suggestions to enhance your resilience:

FORGING A RESILIENT PATH

1. Resilience is the ability to rebound from early adversity and prevail over the circumstances of our lives. Resilient people are able to love well, to work well, and to play well. They may have experienced considerable suffering in their childhood but—often with much difficulty and over a period of many years—they have emerged as better and stronger individuals.

2. They maintain a vision of hope for their future. Whatever their experiences in the past, they believe in the promise of a better tomorrow. They pursue their goals with energy and determination.

3. Resilient people are not exceptional individuals who manifest a rare level of competence. Nor are they invulnerable to the misfortunes in their lives. They are merely ordinary individuals who, given the challenges they have faced, manage to lead fulfilling lives.

4. They do not see themselves as mere survivors who are barely able to cope with their lives. Nor do they see themselves as

passive victims who are tethered to the past, forever mired in the quicksand of their early experiences and unable to derive much pleasure from the present. They use the lessons of the past to live better in the present and assume ownership of their lives and responsibility for their actions.

5. Resilient people have the courage to face their past and have developed a realistic appraisal of its impact on the present. They have accepted the losses of their early years. But that acceptance is not accompanied by bitterness and anger; it is simply their acknowledgement of an imperfect world. They view their own family with understanding, compassion, and generosity.

6. They remember the credo about having the serenity to accept the things they cannot change, the courage to change the things they can, and the wisdom to know the difference. When they have done their best, they channel their energy in new directions.

7. Resilient people view the world and themselves in positive but realistic terms. They look for and acknowledge the strengths in themselves and others, emphasize their gains rather than their losses, and search for the opportunity hidden in adversity. A measured optimism guides their journey through life.

8. At the same time, they can acknowledge the darkness as well as the light, their own shortcomings and those of others, the fragility of human existence, and the reality of injustice and tragedy. When confronted with darkness, they are sustained by their convictions and ideals and by their sense of the world as a meaningful and coherent place.

9. Resilient people are able to reach out to others, to recruit those who can help them in their journey, to offer love and support to others, and to derive satisfaction from their relationships.

(continued on page 140)

10. They face life's challenges with confidence, based on their belief that they can surmount their problems. They actively seek out the information they need, develop the relevant skills, and learn from the experiences of others.

11. Resilient people believe in themselves—in their value, in their abilities, and in their right to a good life. Inevitable setbacks are viewed as temporary. They have learned to do "whatever it takes" to resolve their problems and move on.

12. They hear a call to service, recognizing the limitations of a life lived only for personal pleasure. When their own corner of the world is in disarray, they have learned they can make a difference in the lives of others. Their service to others may take the form of contributions to family and friends, to a cause they believe in, or to the larger society.

Mileposts

The fifth leg of your journey is now complete. At this juncture, you've learned how to:

- enhance your effectiveness in coping with the mental illness in your family and with its impact on your own life;

- develop a Personal Action Plan that can assist you in translating your new insights into constructive change; and

- deal more effectively with the mental health system.

In addition, you've learned how to forge a resilient path, although it's essential to stay flexible in the future. Change is inevitable—for your relative, for your family, and for you. Thus, whatever your plan in the present, you need to remain open to different choices in the future.

You're now ready to embark on the final leg of your journey of hope and healing: renewing your life in the present.

Chapter 7

RENEWING
YOUR LIFE

༄

*I learned that there were some things I had to live with. I know the
cost of mental illness on the soul—and that is very humanizing.
With my father's death, I have learned that I will always remember him, sick or well, and that I can go on doing my best for my
own children. Throughout his illness, he made us feel like we mat-
tered greatly to him. We talk of him often. I think the stories we
tell are a way of living and recovering.*

THESE ARE THE WORDS of one family member who has shared
your journey of hope and healing. In spite of his intimate knowledge of the cost of mental illness, he's made peace with the illness
in his family and established a satisfying and productive life of his own.
He did so without losing sight of the loving father behind the symptoms
of mental illness.

As you begin the final leg of your journey of hope and healing, you've
largely completed the naming and taming of your SaC Syndrome. With
the Personal Action Plan, you've already begun to make constructive
changes in your life. If you're like many family members, as you've re-
vised your legacy and recaptured your energy, you may find yourself
reaching outward—to others inside and outside your family.

LANDMARKS

This leg of your journey includes three prominent landmarks. First, we'll help you chart your course so far. As you review your progress, you'll gain a better sense of where you've been, where you are now, and where you are headed in the future.

Second, if renewal of family bonds is part of your blueprint for the future, we'll provide some assistance. You can build on your new insights, skills, and strategies to establish more fulfilling relationships with all members of your family, including your relative.

Third, we'll help you develop a Family Action Plan that will empower your family in the present and the future. There is much your family can do to cope with the unwelcome and formidable presence in your midst. You may not be able to slay the dragon of mental illness—but you can ensure that it doesn't keep you from living full and satisfying lives.

Perhaps your journey will end at this point, with the naming and taming of your SaC Syndrome, the development of your Personal Action Plan, and the renewal of your family relationships. Or possibly you'll choose to reach out beyond your personal boundaries and to move into an advocacy role. If so, we'll offer some suggestions.

CHARTING YOUR COURSE

You've now completed five legs of your journey of hope and healing. During the first leg, you revisited your childhood to understand the impact of the illness on your early years. You learned about the disruptive effects of mental illness on your family system and on individual family members.

The second leg brought an opportunity to reclaim your childhood. You gained appreciation of your special vulnerability as a young family member, insight into the many ways mental illness has affected your life inside and outside your family, and awareness of your potential for a resilient response to a catastrophic family event.

Beginning with the third leg of your journey, you shifted from the past to the present and discovered the meaning of mental illness for your adulthood. You explored the personal, occupational, interpersonal, and family dimensions of your legacy.

The fourth leg helped you to move beyond understanding and to achieve resolution. You considered your adaptation process, your essential needs as a family member, and the resources that can ease your way.

By the end of the fifth leg, you had begun to revise your legacy, shrinking the SaC Syndrome and placing the mental illness in perspective, as a single event in your life. You learned how to enhance your coping effectiveness, to develop a Personal Action Plan, and to deal more effectively with the mental health system.

Earlier we talked about the three elements of hope: a meaningful goal, willpower, and waypower. Undoubtedly, the first two elements were present when you began reading *How to Cope with Mental Illness in Your Family.* Your goal was to come to terms with the mental illness in your family, and you were highly motivated to achieve this goal. But like family members everywhere, you probably lacked waypower—the path that could guide you toward your goal. We trust we have helped you find that path and move on with your journey. But the accomplishments have been yours; and they have required time, effort, and courage. Before moving on, you need to celebrate your accomplishments. As one family member wrote, "When a family experiences something like this, it makes for very compassionate people. We are people of substance."

At this point, we hope you're able to view your family circumstances as a challenge rather than a threat, to maintain a sense of confidence and hopefulness, and to recognize your gains. But, as you know, this is a lifelong process, one that often involves a step backward for every step forward, and one that is more circular than direct, returning you again and again to the same issues and concerns. You may sometimes feel as if you're riding on a family roller coaster in response both to the course of your relative's mental illness and to the continuing challenges that accompany the illness. Understanding the nature of this lifelong process allows you to anticipate, prepare for, and meet your challenges.

Gradually, you'll be able to rechannel your energy into enriching your life and renewing your family relationships.

RENEWING FAMILY RELATIONSHIPS

As you've progressed with your personal journey, you've also learned about your family's experience with mental illness. You've gained a new appreciation of their struggles, their losses, and their courage. You've developed increased compassion for their suffering and greater respect for their fortitude. You've also acquired more tolerance for human imperfection and more humility regarding your own limitations. You not only see your own life in a new light; you also have a new vision of your family.

Reflecting your new vantage point, you may find yourself ready to renew your family relationships. There are many ingredients in family renewal. One essential ingredient is your personal healing, which allows you to relinquish the anger you may have felt earlier in your life. The following family member describes her changed attitude toward her family: "After being married and having children, I began to come to terms with the anger I felt toward my family." Gradually, she came to understand their terrible burden and their struggle to do the best they could. Ultimately, she was able to respond with empathy rather than anger and to openly discuss their common journey with her family.

Another important ingredient is your family's adaptation, as they move through their own grieving process and accept the reality of the illness in their lives. A third ingredient is the larger context of your family life space, in which the mental illness is simply one event, along with your family triumphs and celebrations. Mental illness doesn't fully capture your family portrait. As this family member attests, a much larger frame is needed to portray the full scope of your lives together—in the past and the future, in good times and bad:

> My brother's illness has only been a part of our family life. My parents were there for me, too, and I felt loved and valued. It was okay for me to be happy. I was never expected to compete with his darkness. My brother lives with my parents and has a job now. He's doing well most of the time. My parents never took the easy way out, never washed their hands of him, never locked him away to get on with their lives. They have provided the support he needs.

A final ingredient is your family's resilience—their ability to surmount their difficulties with love, with grace, and with tenacity. Many family members bear witness to resilience. One affirms: "My brother has created a bond among us all that we will not allow to be broken." Another proclaims: "My family has become more cohesive, much closer, and more communicative since the onset of my brother's mental illness."

It's been suggested that families are like tea bags: The hotter the water, the stronger they become. Listen to this family member:

> There is absolutely nothing each of us wouldn't do for the others. We celebrate the high points and come together in times of trouble. Along with mental illness, we've dealt with divorce, alcoholism, and the routine ups and downs in life. In every instance we relied on each and every one of us, and we come up triumphant. Whatever may be ahead, I know I will never go it alone. I can recall several times when the going got tough, I would tell myself, "Hey, it's okay, my family is there." I feel strengthened with them in my corner.

If you, too, are ready for this process of family renewal, we have some suggestions.

Renewing Family Relationships

1. WHATEVER THE EARLIER TURMOIL, BE OPEN TO NEW BEGINNINGS AND FAMILY RELATIONSHIPS. In reading this book, you've learned about the family experience of mental illness. You've also learned about the unique experiences, needs, and concerns of each individual member. Reveal your wisdom to your family.

2. DISCUSS THE MENTAL ILLNESS WITH YOUR FAMILY, SHARING EXPERIENCES, FEELINGS, NEEDS, AND SUGGESTIONS. Respond to one another with understanding, compassion, and support. Forgive yourself and your family for the omissions and commissions of earlier years.

(continued on page 146)

3. REVISIT THE EARLIER YEARS TOGETHER. Gain validation of your remembered past and learn from the memories and perspectives of your family. Together you may construct a more complete and accurate picture of mutual history.

4. REFLECT ON THE PRESENT TOGETHER. Learn how your family encounter with mental illness was carried on as a legacy in each of your lives, affecting all of your family relationships. Recognize one another's anguish and losses. Also acknowledge your gains as individuals and as a family. Feel pride and satisfaction in your family bonds, strengths, and commitments.

5. PLAN FOR A FUTURE TOGETHER. Place the mental illness in perspective, as simply one of the experiences you've known as a family. Undertake long-term planning for your relative. Also plan for the ongoing life of your family, and for the sharing of future rituals, celebrations, and losses.

6. FULLY MOURN YOUR LOSSES. If you are among those family members who cannot renew original family bonds due to irrevocable losses, such as the death of your relative, fully mourn those losses. Then expand your family to include your friends and others who enrich your life; nurture those relationships.

RECONNECTING WITH YOUR RELATIVE

Perhaps you've been able to maintain a satisfying and loving relationship with your relative throughout the painful years with mental illness. More likely, your relationship has been troubling for both of you. Whatever the problems of the past, however, you have an opportunity in the present to establish a more constructive relationship with your relative that acknowledges your family bonds and that respects your differing strengths, limitations, needs, and rights. In the words of one family member, "I accept people as they are. People can be loving and valuable even if they don't live according to society's standard of success."

As you reconnect with your relative, you need to focus on the human being behind the symptoms. Describing her feelings about her brother, the following woman conveys this overriding sense of our common humanity:

> The mental illness is not my real brother, but is like an added-on thing. I always really liked the person he is—sensitive, very intelligent, creative, entertaining, and interesting. He's a very good person, honest and caring. Knowing my brother has given me more compassion and a better understanding of social problems like homelessness. In certain ways, we are all better people for having known my brother.

Looking beyond the mental illness, many family members told us about their cherished bond with their relative. One family member wrote, "I know that despite my mother's illness, she really did love me and still does. That is a gift that enabled me to grow into a whole person." A sibling described a journey that carried him through the depths of his brother's mental illness and the devastation of homelessness. As real as these events were, so too are his brother's strengths: "When he is well, he is a person with unlimited compassion for other people."

In addition, we heard about the pride experienced by family members in response to their relatives' achievements. One man wrote: "My mother is doing very well. I'm very proud of her, the things she does as an advocate. She is leading as meaningful a life as she can." Another family member echoed his pride: "My mother has moved to a new state and enjoys exploring the history and environment. She has a renewed interest in current events. This active, intellectual involvement seems to keep her healthy." We also learned about the contributions of people with mental illness to their families. A sibling talked about her brother's positive influence on her daughter: "She will grow up to realize that different people are all right."

Earlier we described the legacy of mental illness for your life. This legacy—the SaC Syndrome—has undoubtedly imprinted your life in profound ways. But there is another kind of legacy as well, one that should also command our attention. This very different legacy proclaims: People with mental illness enrich our lives. After all, the ranks of people with mental illness include Abraham Lincoln and Winston Churchill, Mark Twain and Ernest Hemingway, Michelangelo and Vincent van

Gogh, and Handel and Tchaikovsky. These ranks also include individuals whose contributions are closer to home:

> My father taught us to love each other—he was the best hugger I ever met. He loved my mom and all of us. He loved nature and taught us about trees, gardening, and caring for pets. He spent time with us going for walks, singing, playing cards, and reading stories. He taught us songs. He was a happy, caring person who uplifted those who came in contact with him.

If you are ready to reconnect with your relative, here are some suggestions:

RECONNECTING WITH YOUR RELATIVE

1. LEARN ABOUT YOUR RELATIVE'S EXPERIENCE OF SERIOUS MENTAL ILLNESS. For example, ask your relative what is it like to hear voices, to be hypersensitive to sights and sounds, to have difficulty thinking logically and rationally, to believe people are controlling one's thoughts, or to experience extreme mood swings. Personal accounts by people with mental illness are helpful (see Appendix A).

2. ACKNOWLEDGE YOUR RELATIVE'S SOMETIMES HEROIC STRUGGLE. Treat him or her with respect, dignity, and compassion. Ask about the ongoing struggle with mental illness and about the coping strategies that are most helpful. Remember that your relative is not synonymous with the illness, but has the same needs, hopes, and dreams shared by all of us.

3. MAINTAIN A POSITIVE ATTITUDE AND ACKNOWLEDGE YOUR RELATIVE'S POTENTIAL FOR GROWTH AND RECOVERY. Along with the mental illness, your relative has strengths and gifts; encourage his or her contributions.

4. PLAY A CONSTRUCTIVE ROLE IN YOUR RELATIVE'S LIFE. Provide information, advice, support, and companionship.

You may be able to help your relative come to terms with his or her illness. People with mental illness often say that accepting the fact of their illness was one of the most difficult tasks of their lives. At the same time, learning that your problem is an illness can be a relief.

5. HELP YOUR RELATIVE WITH SPECIFIC PROBLEMS. Ask your relative how you can be helpful when he or she is dealing with the symptoms of the illness, difficulties within the family, limited social life, or other concerns. Work together to establish reasonable household rules, to avoid crises and relapses, to solve personal and family problems, and to plan for the future.

6. MAINTAIN A VISION OF HOPE AND RECOVERY. People with mental illness enrich our lives. All of them have the potential for recovery and an improved quality of life. Celebrate your human bond with your relative, share in life's pleasures, and during difficult times hope for a better tomorrow.

We've talked about renewing family relationships and reconnecting with your relative. Together with the rest of your family, you can develop a Family Action Plan that will help you prevail over the difficult circumstances of your lives.

DEVELOPING A FAMILY ACTION PLAN

If you are like most family members, you may have little sense that a Family Action Plan is even a possibility against such a formidable opponent. But there is much that your family can do under these circumstances. In the following sections, we'll share some suggestions that have helped many other families who are coping with the mental illness of a close relative.

There are some excellent resources to assist you and your family. We have included brief descriptions of many of them in Appendix A. Some of the best books and sources of information include The Journey of Hope Family Education and Support Program developed by Joyce Burland and Donna Mayeux (contact your state NAMI office); *Coping with Schizophrenia: A Guide for Families* by Kim Mueser and Susan Gingerich; *Surviving Schizophrenia: A Manual for Consumers, Families and Providers* by E. Fuller Torrey; and *When Someone You Love Has a Mental Illness: A Handbook* by Rebecca Woolis.

Before moving on to specific suggestions, we want to emphasize two important considerations. First, whatever the situation at home, never lose sight of your own needs, hopes, and dreams. In fact, the greater the disruption resulting from your relative's mental illness, the more important it is for you to take care of yourself. Don't let the mental illness take over your life!

Second, remember that you cannot live your relative's life—the only life you can live is your own. It may be helpful to recall the credo about having the serenity to accept the things you cannot change, the courage to change the things you can, and the wisdom to know the difference. When you have done your best, channel your energy into your own life and the larger world. Even when you are feeling helpless about your personal circumstances, you can make a difference in the lives of others.

Responding to a Catastrophic Event

1. The mental illness of a close relative confronts all families with a challenge of enormous proportions. The initial response of most family members is often a paralyzing sense of disbelief, confusion, helplessness, and hopelessness. Yet your family already has some strengths for coping with this challenge. No one has a better understanding of your family or shares your lifetime commitment to your relative.

2. Under these circumstances your family also needs to obtain new knowledge about your relative's mental illness and its treatment, to acquire new skills for coping with the illness and the mental health system, and to find new sources of support. A major goal of *How to Cope with Mental Illness in Your Family* has been to help you develop these new strengths.

3. Initially, it may be helpful to establish a family team that consists of all members of the family, including your relative, whose recovery will be enhanced by playing an active and informed role in decisions about treatment and rehabilitation. Young members of the family also need to feel they are a part of the process.

4. Responsibilities of family members should reflect their particular roles, ages, concerns, and circumstances. For example, adult members of the family need to ensure that young family members do not move into "parentified" roles; young siblings and offspring need support for their own growth and development. At the same time, young family members need information in terms they can understand, opportunities to share their feelings and concerns, and assistance in coping.

5. It is essential for your family to work collaboratively with the professional team that is treating your relative. Professionals can help your family learn about your relative's recovery process, develop appropriate expectations, and respond to early warning signs of relapse. In addition, they can help your family cope with specific problems, such as medication compliance, substance abuse, and the risk of self-destructive or violent behavior.

6. Although crises demand an immediate and focused response, on a long-term basis your family should aim to maintain a normal family lifestyle, reestablish family routines, and continue with customary activities. Your family can strive for a balance that meets the needs of all members of the family, that encourages their growth and development, and that improves their quality of life. This is often easier said than done!

Providing a Supportive Environment

1. People with mental illness are unusually vulnerable to stress. Events that are barely noticed by others may overwhelm them. Thus, your relative can benefit from a low-key environment and an opportunity for a time-out when things get hectic.

2. Your relative may be especially sensitive to interpersonal friction. Avoid unnecessary criticism and conflict and learn to express your concerns in a nonjudgmental way. Use "I Messages" ("I can't do my work when the music is so loud.") rather than "You Messages" ("You never think about anyone else and are rude to play your music so loud.").

3. Mental illness sometimes makes it difficult for your relative to communicate effectively. You can help by listening attentively, responding empathically, speaking clearly and directly, and keeping messages brief and straightforward.

4. Your family can benefit from good problem-solving skills. In a given situation, these skills can help in defining and analyzing the problem, in generating and evaluating solutions, and in selecting and implementing a solution. If the chosen solution does not result in satisfactory resolution of the problem, the process may begin again.

5. Given the confusion and disorganization that often accompany mental illness, your relative can also benefit from an environment that offers structure, stability, and consistency. When change is necessary or desirable, it can be facilitated by open discussion, careful planning, and a pace that is comfortable for your relative.

6. A constructive atmosphere can improve your family's ability to cope with the mental illness. Such an atmosphere is characterized by open and direct communication, by mutual tolerance and respect, and by caring, commitment, and affection. Differences can then be resolved in a way that acknowledges the perspectives of all family members and results in a mutually acceptable solution.

Learning to Set Limits

1. Limit setting is important for all family members. No one should have to live in a dangerous or disturbing environment.

2. Certain behaviors are not acceptable and should not be tolerated. These include behavior that is abusive, self-destructive, harmful to others, damaging to property, or severely disruptive. You need to decide which behaviors are unacceptable, set clear limits, and impose consequences when those limits are exceeded.

3. It is also important to decide which behaviors can be ignored. For example, behavior that may harm your relative or others is more important than behavior that is merely annoying or embarrassing.

4. It is best to discuss these issues with your relative prior to a crisis. Many problems can be avoided through advance planning. It may be helpful to have a written contract that lists unacceptable behaviors and the actions that will be taken by family members if those behaviors occur.

5. Limits should be based on reasonable expectations for all members of the family. Those expectations should reflect their ages, their roles in the family, and their strengths and limitations.

6. Learn to set personal limits. Don't let the mental illness of your relative overpower your own needs and goals. The illness needs to be placed in perspective—as a single event in your entire life, which encompasses a wide range of experiences, relationships, challenges, and opportunities. Maintain a comfortable level of involvement in your relative's life that allows you to fully live your own life.

Dealing with Positive Symptoms

1. The symptoms of serious mental illness are sometimes divided into positive and negative symptoms. Positive symptoms involve exaggeration or distortion of normal functions. Examples include hallucinations (false perceptions), such as hearing voices; delusions (false beliefs), such as a conviction that one is

being persecuted; disorganized thought and speech; and bizarre behavior.

2. It is useful to remember that people with mental illness experience hallucinations and delusions as real, although with time they may learn to recognize these experiences as symptoms of their disorder. It is not helpful to argue with them about the reality of their hallucinations and delusions. You are not likely to convince them they are wrong, and the conflict will be stressful for both of you.

3. It is best to respond in a way that respects their dignity without reinforcing their symptoms.

4. You can remain nonjudgmental (avoid challenging his or her statement) while responding to your relative's concerns. For example, you may choose to acknowledge what you have heard ("That's very interesting."), to offer support ("I'm sure that must upset you."), to convey empathy ("I'd be worried too if I heard those voices."), to offer assistance ("Can I do anything to make you feel better?"), or to change the subject ("Let's go for a walk.").

5. Remember that your relative may suffer considerably from the hallucinations and delusions that often accompany serious mental illness. What may be annoying for you can be terrifying for your relative.

6. You may wish to consult with your relative's therapist or case manager regarding the best way to handle positive symptoms in his or her case.

Dealing with Negative Symptoms

1. Negative symptoms involve a decrease in or loss of normal thoughts, experiences, and feelings. Such symptoms may include apathy and inability to follow through on tasks; inability to experience pleasure and to enjoy relationships; inability to feel and express emotions; inability to focus on activities; and impoverished thought and speech.

2. Learn to recognize these symptoms as part of the illness and to develop realistic expectations for your relative. Struggling with mental illness may consume much of your relative's time and energy.

3. As difficult as it may be for you to observe the limitations of your relative's life, it is also difficult to live such a life, which may seem barren and meaningless.

4. Offer your relative an opportunity to talk about his or her negative symptoms and discuss possible strategies for improving task performance. Rehabilitation may offer an opportunity to improve skills, functioning, and life satisfaction. In addition, some newer medications appear to lessen negative symptoms.

5. Encourage your relative to engage in new social activities. Many communities have drop-in centers and support groups for people with mental illness. As with the rest of the family, your relative may benefit from contact with others who have had similar experiences and who can offer hope and advice during difficult periods.

6. You may wish to consult with your relative's therapist or case manager regarding the best way to handle negative symptoms in his or her case.

Coping with Crises

1. Learn the warning signs of impending crisis. Warning signs may include sudden changes in behavior, hallucinations or delusions, disorganized speech or thinking, bizarre behavior, verbal threats, changes in eating or sleeping patterns, or fluctuations in activity level or mood.

2. Be prepared. Have contingency plans ready and keep emergency phone numbers available. You may find it helpful to discuss these plans with your relative in advance. Your plans should include a list of people who can offer assistance in a cri-

sis. These may include other family members, friends, neighbors, professionals, or the police.

3. During a crisis, your relative is likely to be confused, overwhelmed, and unfocused. Remain calm yourself and give your relative an opportunity to calm down. Your own behavior is likely to have a major impact on your relative during a crisis. Avoid threatening, shouting, criticizing, or arguing with other family members. Separate the person from the symptoms, which may include anger directed at you. Don't take it personally. A brief time-out may be best for everyone.

4. Approach the crisis in a firm, straightforward, loving, and respectful manner. Comply with reasonable requests that are not harmful to your relative or to others; this can increase your relative's sense of control and support. Attend to the physical environment. Encourage everyone to sit down (it is less threatening), minimize direct eye contact and physical contact with your relative (both can increase stress), and avoid cornering or restricting your relative (which can increase the risk of harm).

5. Medication compliance is generally an essential part of treatment and is likely to reduce the risk of relapse and crisis. People with mental illness may refuse to take medication because they do not accept their illness, are experiencing symptoms that interfere with treatment, or dislike the side effects.

6. Calmly discuss these issues with your relative, offer relevant educational materials, and work with professionals in increasing the likelihood of medication compliance. Strategies include using injectables, the lowest effective dosage, and the medication most acceptable to your relative. Promising new medications have become available in recent years; others are currently in development.

Managing Potentially Self-Destructive Behavior

1. People who attempt suicide often show warning signs. These may include expressions of hopelessness or helplessness;

changes in biological functions, such as eating or sleeping; severe mood changes; withdrawal from usual activities; final arrangements, such as giving away possessions or writing a will; suicidal threats, especially if there is a suicide plan; hallucinations that encourage a suicide attempt; or an expressed wish to die. Prior suicidal thoughts, gestures, or attempts increase the risk associated with any of these signs.

2. Do not ignore the signs of potentially self-destructive behavior. That may encourage this behavior, lead to further escalation, or increase the likelihood of harm to your relative. Stay calm, show concern and empathy, and remain available to talk.

3. Ask your relative if he or she is thinking about suicide. Such an approach may offer the opportunity to better understand your relative's state of mind, to prevent self-destructive behavior, and to obtain professional assistance. Also ask if your relative has a suicide plan, which is considered a significant risk factor.

4. Encourage your relative to get professional help. If necessary, seek professional assistance yourself. Contact a mental health professional, a suicide prevention center, or the police.

5. Consider using an advance directive if there has been prior self-destructive behavior. An advance directive allows your relative to specify preferred treatment decisions if he or she is not capable of making an informed choice. Petition for an involuntary commitment if your relative has committed any self-destructive acts and you cannot get assistance in any other way.

6. Someone who is determined to die may ultimately be successful. You cannot always prevent suicide and should not feel responsible if you are faced with this tragic loss.

Managing Potentially Violent Behavior

1. Learn the warning signs of potentially violent behavior. These may include expressions of hostility; harmful threats, especially if there is a violent plan; hallucinations that encourage violence; or a paranoid delusion that one is being watched, persecuted, or attacked. The best predictor of future violence is a history of violence, which increases the risk associated with any of these signs.

2. Do not ignore the signs of potentially violent behavior. Such a stance may encourage the behavior, lead to further escalation, or increase the likelihood of harm to your relative or others. Whatever your inner turmoil, try to respond in a calm, accepting, and respectful manner. Offer concrete suggestions that can defuse the situation.

3. Tell your relative that his or her behavior is frightening you. Sometimes this can lessen the risk of harm and help your relative understand the impact of his or her behavior on other people.

4. Avoid lectures, criticism, verbal threats, and hostile remarks. These are likely to further upset your relative and increase the risk of harm.

5. Leave the scene immediately if you feel in danger. Get assistance from the police or other appropriate parties.

6. Consider using an advance directive if there has been prior violent behavior. Petition for an involuntary commitment if your relative has committed any violent acts and you cannot get assistance in any other way.

Dealing with Alcohol and Drug Abuse

Alcohol and drug abuse are frequent problems among people with mental illness. For example, at some point in their lives almost 50 percent of people who have schizophrenia also develop a substance-abuse disorder, as do 30 percent of those with depression, manic depression, or other mood disorders. When a person suffers from both mental illness and substance abuse, it is called a dual diagnosis.

Family members face special challenges when their relative carries a dual diagnosis. For all people with a substance abuse problem, there are harmful effects on health, relationships, and work. When a mental illness is present, substance abuse can result in exacerbation of symptoms and increase the risk of relapse and hospitalization. Even when your relative is receiving substance-abuse treatment, the risk of relapse is high and recovery often involves repeated efforts and long-term treatment.

Learn about your relative's use of alcohol and drugs. People with mental illness generally abuse substances for three reasons: (a) to temporarily reduce symptoms and side effects of medication through self-medication; (b) to enhance their social life and reduce their feelings of isolation; and (c) to increase pleasant feelings (or at least reduce unpleasant ones) as an antidote to the anguish and loss associated with mental illness. In severe cases, substances are used to prevent withdrawal symptoms or cravings. These are all powerful reinforcers.

Keep the channel of communication open with your relative. When you are not in the midst of a crisis, discuss the substance use calmly, nonjudgmentally, and compassionately. Talk about the advantages and disadvantages of substance use. Express your concern and try to understand your relative's perspective.

On a long-term basis, try to persuade your relative that the substance abuse is a problem (denial is common). Encourage your relative to get help and to find better ways of meeting his or her needs. These might include participation in structured activities, involvement in a self-help group (such as a mental health consumer group or Alcoholics Anonymous), or professional substance-abuse treatment. Ultimately, however, these steps must be taken by your relative.

You may wish to consult with your relative's therapist or case manager to develop a plan that meets the needs of all members of the family. Establish household rules (for example, no substance abuse in the home) and consider alternative living arrangements if your relative cannot conform to the rules. Develop a list of resources for your relative with names and phone numbers, such as an intensive case manager, another family member or consumer who is willing to serve as a resource, a consumer self-help group, or a member of Alcoholics Anonymous.

Planning for the Future

By definition, serious mental illness involves severe and persistent disabilities in multiple areas of functioning. People with these disabilities need long-term support, which in turn requires long-term planning. Thus, it is essential for families to have an open and continuing dialogue regarding plans for their relative and to consult with experts who can assist them. To the extent possible, your relative should play an active role in decisions that affect his or her future.

People with serious mental illness are generally eligible for a range of benefits, including Social Security Disability Insurance (SSDI), Supplementary Security Income (SSI), and public assistance (welfare), as well as associated health care and other benefits. Contact your local Social Security office or department of public welfare for further information. Your family needs to ensure that long-term plans do not jeopardize eligibility for these benefits.

Community resources are an essential component for your family. A local case manager can serve as your relative's advocate, coordinate mental health and other important services, and keep your family informed about residential living arrangements in your community. Sometimes these functions are performed by family members, such as parents of an adult son or daughter who resides at home. As they age, parents need to develop a community network that can meet the needs of their relative on a continuing basis. Such a network is essential for siblings who do not reside locally.

Long-term planning also involves family resources. Contact a lawyer who is knowledgeable about estate planning for people with mental illness and who can meet regularly with your family. If your family wishes to provide for your relative's future without jeopardizing his or her eligibility for benefits, you may wish to establish a trust fund and appoint a trustee to administer the trust. The trustee, either an individual or financial institution, distributes funds based on the specific provisions of the trust.

Your family can also benefit from other resources, both locally and nationally. For instance, NAMI can provide information about the Planned Lifetime Assistance Network (PLAN). Finally, depending on the age and capacities of your relative, your family may need to become familiar with procedures for establishing health-care proxy (concerned with treatment decisions) and durable power of attorney (concerned with legal and financial matters); and for appointment of a guardian (with authority over personal and financial decisions) or conservator (with authority over property and money issues).

REACHING OUT

Now that you've reached the end of your journey and have begun to renew your family relationships, you may wish to expand your personal and family boundaries. "Going public" as a family member of someone with mental illness can be both frightening and liberating. After so many years of maintaining your silence, you may feel no small amount of trepidation when you first begin to talk about your "family secret." But once you begin to break your silence, you'll probably connect with others who have shared the family experience of mental illness. And you'll certainly find a valuable source of support among people who care about you—but have had little sense of the turmoil below your placid surface.

Equally important, you'll recapture your energy for more productive use. Keeping a family secret steals precious energy from your life, as does your fear that others will discover the "terrible truth" about you. Once you begin to tell your story, you'll find the truth is not so terrible after all. In the bright daylight, armed with your new insights and skills, you'll be able to confront the true enemy: the corrosive effects of stigma. Rex talks about his own process of reaching out and offers some suggestions:

> Begin slowly. As you realize the value of warmth and understanding, of building interpersonal bridges, it becomes progressively easier. After a while, the "secret" loses its grip and simply becomes information about your family background. I introduced the subject of mental illness in my family by mentioning to a few coworkers that one of my outside interests was writing. Inevitably, they asked what I wrote about. I responded that I had an older brother with schizophrenia. It turned out that several coworkers had mental illness in their families. My apprehension about sharing my story was unjus-

tified. In reality, our shared family experience of mental illness warmed and deepened my relationships with my coworkers.

Moving beyond your personal circle, you may choose to become an advocate—someone who works publicly to improve the quality of life for people with serious mental illness. Of course, not all family members become advocates. But if you do join forces with others in working for a more humane and responsive system of care, there are many potential benefits. These include immediate benefits for your relative as a result of improvements in your local mental health system, as well as personal satisfaction from family-supported developments on state and national levels. Increasingly, family members are joined in advocacy activities by people with mental illness themselves, who are serving as their own advocates for the first time in history.

As you resolve your own issues and renegotiate your family relationships, you may find yourself ready to reach out to other family members. You may wish to share what you have learned, to help them on their journey of hope and healing, and to join forces with them in advocacy. As someone who grew up with mental illness in your family, you'll undoubtedly have a special mission: addressing the needs of the young children who continue to suffer as you suffered, whose needs continue to be neglected, and whose SaC Syndrome continues to reverberate throughout their lives. As a society, we must strengthen our efforts to meet the needs of *all* members of the family. In the words of one family member: "There are many children out there who are suffering the way that my sisters and brother and I suffered. There has to be a way to reach them."

We invite you to contact us: to tell us about your experiences, to offer your suggestions, and to comment on *How to Cope with Mental Illness in Your Family*. We can be reached as follows: Diane T. Marsh, Ph.D., University of Pittsburgh at Greensburg, Greensburg, PA 15601.

We would love to hear from you.

Appendix A

RESOURCES

❧

A LL OF THE RESOURCES listed are available to the general public; however, some may take greater time and effort to locate than others. If a book is still in print, it can be purchased at a local book store or specially ordered. Libraries have access to books both in print and out of print. If your local library does not have them, request the assistance of the reference librarian. Most libraries are linked with a library system.

The National Alliance for the Mentally Ill (NAMI) has many resources available at discounted prices. For a copy of their *Resource Catalog,* contact NAMI at 200 North Glebe Road, Suite 1015, Arlington, VA 22203-3754. Phone: 703-524-7600. In addition, your local or state NAMI affiliate may have some books and videotapes. You can also contact NAMI through e-mail (namiofc@.com) or on the Internet (http:// www.nami.org/). NAMI can inform you about the World Wide Web sites for siblings and offspring, as well as other relevant sites.

The following books and videotapes represent some of the best resources for families. Still other books, articles, and videotapes are listed in *Anguished Voices.* If you would like additional suggestions, feel free to contact us; we are constantly updating our list. We have organized the resources into the following categories:

- siblings and offspring: personal accounts;
- siblings and offspring: nonfiction;

- siblings and offspring: fiction;

- serious mental illness: general information;

- serious mental illness: personal accounts by consumers and parents;

- family coping;

- families: books for professionals;

- young readers;

- youngest readers;

- videotapes and films;

- videotapes for young viewers; and

- organizations.

SIBLINGS AND OFFSPRING: PERSONAL ACCOUNTS

Dickens, R. M., and D. T. Marsh (Eds.). (1994). *Anguished Voices.* Boston: Boston University Center for Psychiatric Rehabilitation. Order the book from the Center: 730 Commonwealth Ave., Boston, MA 02215. 617-353-3549. $10.00. Also available from NAMI.

A companion volume to *How to Cope with Mental Illness in Your Family.* Includes powerful personal accounts by three adult siblings, three adult offspring, and two multigenerational family members. The contributors generously allowed us to use brief excerpts from these accounts in *How to Cope with Mental Illness in Your Family.*

The JOURNAL of the California Alliance for the Mentally Ill. (1992). Sibling issue, Vol. 3, No. 1. Contains articles by and about siblings. (1996). Offspring issue, Vol. 7, No. 3. Contains articles by and about offspring. In addition to the two issues on siblings and offspring, *The JOURNAL* is an excellent resource in the area of serious mental illness. Yearly subscription is $25.00 from the The JOURNAL, 1111 Howe Avenue, Suite 475, Sacramento, CA 95825. 916-567-0163. All prior issues are available.

Karr, M. (1995). *The Liars' Club.* New York: Viking.

A bestselling account of life by an offspring. Provides a vivid recollection of a Texas childhood with a "nervous" mother and a devoted alcoholic father.

Moorman, M. (1992). *My Sister's Keeper.* New York: Norton.

A well-written account by a sibling. Describes her sister's manic depression, her caregiving role following her parents' death, and her emotional journey.

Neugeboren, J. (1997). *Imagining Robert: My Brother, Madness, and Survival.* New York: William Morrow.

With eloquence and compassion, Jay reflects on his brother, himself, and their family, and reminds us of the humanity of one individual embedded in serious mental illness.

Olseon, L. (1994). *He Was Still My Daddy.* Portland, OR: Ogden House.

An account by a woman who chronicles her adolescent years with her father's psychosis. Portrays the emotional isolation, confusion, and ambivalence that often accompany the offspring experience.

Paterson, J. (1996). *Sweet Mystery: A Book of Remembering.* New York: Farrar, Straus, & Giroux.

The account an offspring who was nine when her mother died at age thirty-one from a combination of mental illness and alcohol abuse. Chronicled against a backdrop of small-town life in the rural South.

Sexton, L. (1994). *Searching for Mercy Street: My Journey Back to My Mother, Anne Sexton.* Boston: Little, Brown.

A courageous, eloquent, and searingly honest account of life with her mother, the poet Anne Sexton, who won the Pulitzer Prize. Describes her mother's manic depression and suicide in 1974.

Swados, E. (1991). *The Four of Us.* New York: Farrar, Straus, & Giroux.

A family memoir by a sibling. Explores her brother's schizophrenia, her family dynamics, and their individual and collective journeys.

SIBLINGS AND OFFSPRING: NONFICTION

Anthony, E., and B. Cohler. (Eds.). (1987). *The Invulnerable Child.* New York: Guilford.

A professional book that deals with the legacy of being raised by a parent with mental illness. Contains some early research on resilience.

Brown, E. (1989). *My Parent's Keeper: Adult Children of the Emotionally Disturbed.* Oakland, CA: New Harbinger.

Examines the offspring experience, especially the role of parentified child. Considers other aspects of the experience, including loss of feelings, the need for control, the deep sense of aloneness, and low self-esteem.

Johnson, J. (1988). *Hidden Victims.* New York: Doubleday.

Focuses on family members—the hidden victims of mental illness. Provides an insightful analysis of family concerns and outlines an eight-stage healing process.

Wasow, M. (1995). *The Skipping Stone: Ripple Effects of Mental Illness on the Family.* Palo Alto, CA: Science and Behavior Books.

Offers a description of the impact of mental illness on all members of the family. Based on interviews with family members and written by a professor of social work who has a son with schizophrenia.

SIBLINGS AND OFFSPRING: FICTION

Gibbons, K. (1995). *Sights Unseen.* New York: Putnam.

A twelve-year-old daughter's memoir about her mother's manic-depressive illness. Examines how the illness affected all members of the family.

Roiphe, A. (1993). *If You Knew Me.* Boston: Little, Brown.

Describes the relationship between a sibling and an offspring who find each other later in life. Explores their individual legacies, as he learns to take care of his own emotional needs and she learns to trust someone besides herself.

Vandenburgh, J. (1989). *Failure to Zigzag*. San Francisco: North Point Press.

The story of an adolescent offspring. Describes her encounter with her mother's mental illness and her own travails before liberation.

SERIOUS MENTAL ILLNESS: GENERAL INFORMATION

Andreasen, N. (Ed.). (1994). *Schizophrenia: From Mind to Molecule*. Washington, DC: American Psychiatric Press.

A clear and informed examination of schizophrenia. Covers the human experience, phenomenology, neurobiology, treatment, and future directions.

Gorman, J. (1995). *The Essential Guide to Psychiatric Drugs*. New York: St. Martin's Paperbacks.

Offers an update of a bestselling introduction to psychiatric medication. Basic information on drugs used to treat depression, anxiety, bipolar disorder, schizophrenia, sleep disorders, and substance abuse.

Gottesman, I. (1990). *Schizophrenia Genesis: The Origins of Madness*. New York: W. H. Freeman.

Presents current views on the genetics in schizophrenia by a leading researcher. Examines the genetic risks for family members.

Hatfield, A., and H. Lefley. (1993). *Surviving Mental Illness*. New York: Guilford.

Explores the subjective experiences of people with serious mental illness, including schizophrenia, bipolar disorder, and major depression. Offers an essential perspective on what it is like to have a serious mental illness.

Hershman, J., and J. Leib. (1988). *The Key to Genius: Manic Depression and the Creative Life*. Buffalo, NY: Prometheus Books.

An insightful book on manic depression. Explores the role of manic depression in the creative lives of Newton, Beethoven, and Dickens.

Keefe, R., and P. Harvey. (1994). *Understanding Schizophrenia: A Guide to the New Research on Causes and Treatment.* New York: Free Press.

Provides an excellent overview of schizophrenia, its neurobiological causes, and current treatment approaches. Written in a reader-friendly manner that makes it an excellent resource for families.

Torrey, E. F., A. Bowler, E. Taylor, and I. Gottesman. (1994). *Schizophrenia and Manic-Depressive Disorder.* New York: Basic Books.

Presents results of a six-year study of schizophrenia and bipolar disorder in sixty-six pairs of identical twins. Offers a comprehensive and research-based look at the biological roots of schizophrenia and manic depression.

Serious Mental Illness: Personal Accounts by Consumers and Parents

Berger, D., and L. Berger. (1991). *We Heard the Angels of Madness: One Family's Struggle with Manic Depression.* New York: Morrow.

A personal account of one family's experience with manic depression. Offers a useful overview of the illness and its treatment.

Cronkite, K. (1994). *On the Edge of Darkness: Conversations About Conquering Depression.* New York: Doubleday.

A series of interviews with well-known individuals, such as Joan Rivers and Mike Wallace, who discuss their personal experiences with depression. Includes interviews with professionals who examine the illness and its treatment.

Deveson, A. (1992). *Tell Me I'm Here: One Family's Experience of Schizophrenia.* New York: Penguin Books.

A powerful account of a son's schizophrenia and his mother's anguish. Charts her experiences with the mental health system, as well as her son's deteriorating course and eventual suicide.

Jamison, K. (1995). *An Unquiet Mind: A Memoir of Moods and Madness.* New York: Knopf.

A personal account by a psychologist and authority on mood disorders. Inarguably one of the most powerful, insightful, and eloquent depictions of life with manic depression.

Schiller, L., and A. Bennett. (1994). *The Quiet Room.* New York: Warner.

A personal account by a woman who has schizophrenia. Describes its devastating impact on her life and her family, as well as her recovery process.

Thompson, T. (1995). *The Beast: A Reckoning with Depression.* New York: Putnam.

A well-written personal account of a long struggle with depression by a reporter for *The Washington Post.* Offers a valuable perspective on life with "the beast" and strategies for coping.

Wechsler, J. (1988). *In a Darkness* (2nd ed.). Miami: Pickering.

A veteran journalist chronicles his son's mental illness and eventual suicide. Recounts his frustrating experiences with professionals and his family's anguish.

Family Coping

Backlar, P. (1994). *The Family Face of Schizophrenia.* New York: Tarcher/Putnam.

A series of narratives about families who have a member with schizophrenia. Following each narrative, experts offer advice on the issues raised in the story, including sibling concerns.

Burland, J., and D. Mayeux. (1996). *The Journey of Hope Family Support and Education Program.* Available through NAMI and its state affiliates.

The family education program covers serious mental illness, family concerns, and coping skills. The family support program offers training for facilitators of support groups for family members.

Mueser, K., and S. Gingerich. (1994). *Coping with Schizophrenia: A Guide for Families.* Oakland, CA: New Harbinger.

A comprehensive and practical guide to coping with mental illness. Offers a wealth of information and provides step-by-step assistance for dealing with a wide range of problems.

Rosen, L., and X. Amador. (1996). *When Someone You Love Is Depressed: How to Help Your Loved One Without Losing Yourself.* New York: Free Press.
   Focuses on the family members or partners of people who have depression. Emphasizes what they can do for themselves and for their loved one.

Torrey, E. F. (1995). *Surviving Schizophrenia: A Manual for Families, Consumers and Providers* (3rd ed.). New York: HarperCollins.
   A bestselling book by a leading researcher that deals comprehensively with schizophrenia. Offers practical suggestions for all those affected by mental illness and a comprehensive list of resources.

Woolis, R. (1992). *When Someone You Love Has a Mental Illness: A Handbook.* New York: Tarcher/Perigee.
   Provides forty-three "Quick Reference Guides" to enhance family coping. Suggestions offered for dealing with hallucinations, delusions, violence, and medication compliance, as well as choosing residences, doctors, and treatment plans.

FAMILIES: BOOKS FOR PROFESSIONALS

Lefley, H. (1996). *Family Caregiving in Mental Illness.* Thousand Oaks, CA: Sage.
   A comprehensive overview of roles families play in caring for relatives with mental illness. Discusses historical perspectives, different family members, and life-cycle issues.

Lefley, H., and M. Wasow. (Eds.). (1994). *Helping Families Cope with Mental Illness.* Newark: Harwood Academic Publishers.
   An outstanding professional book that covers family-professional relationships, services for families, training and research, and future directions. Includes material on siblings and offspring.

Marsh, D. (1992). *Families and Mental Illness: New Directions in Professional Practice.* New York: Praeger.

A professional book that emphasizes the importance of collaboration between family members and professionals. Covers issues and concerns of siblings and offspring.

Young Readers

Adler, C. (1983). *The Shell Lady's Daughter.* New York: Coward-McCann.

While fourteen-year-old Kelly's mother is hospitalized for depression, she stays with her grandparents and resolves struggles about her own emotional needs.

Bridges, S. (1981). *Notes for Another Life.* New York: Knopf.

Living with their grandparents, fourteen-year-old Wren and sixteen-year-old Kevin deal with new loves, family relationships, and internal conflicts, as their father's mental health deteriorates and he returns to the hospital.

Caseley, J. (1992). *My Father, the Nut Case.* New York: Knopf.

Sassy fifteen-year-old Zoe is becoming conscious of many things—her body, boys, family, friendship, and her father's clinical depression.

Cooney, C. (1986). *Don't Blame the Music.* New York: Pacer.

Susan eagerly looks forward to her senior year in high school, but finds her expectations shattered by the return home of her troubled older sister.

Coret, H. (1982). *In and Out the Windows.* Syracuse, NY: New Readers Press.

Misunderstanding abounds among her teachers, parents, boyfriend, and sister as Kit hears and acts on voices no one else hears. We learn about the source of her voices—schizophrenia—and about her inner experience of mental illness.

Corcoran, B. (1990). *Annie's Monster*. New York: Macmillan.

Thirteen-year-old Annie, her monstrous Irish Wolfhound, a distressed outcast with mental illness named Cora, a small community, and her family intermix in this entertaining, knowledgeable story. Emphasizes compassion over indifference.

Hyland, B. (1987). *The Girl with the Crazy Brother*. New York: Watts.

A sophomore in high school, Dana finds herself torn between her love for her brother, the reaction of her friends, and concerns for herself.

Johnson, J. (1989). *Understanding Mental Illness*. Minneapolis: Lerner.

A book for teens, that addresses their fears when a sibling or parent has a mental disorder.

Joosse, B. (1992). *Anna and the Cat Lady*. New York: HarperCollins.

A compassionate introduction to the unusual behavior of a person with paranoid schizophrenia. Nine-year-old Anna develops a friendship with Mrs. Sarafiny, an older woman with many cats and the conviction that the Martians are after her.

Naylor, P. (1986). *The Keeper*. New York: Atheneum.

Sixteen-year-old Nick struggles to get help for his father, who manifests increasingly bizarre behavior.

Riley, J. (1982). *Only My Mouth Is Smiling*. (1984). *Crazy Quilt*. New York: William Morrow.

In the initial book, thirteen-year-old Merle increasingly hides her feelings about her mother's bizarre behavior. In the sequel, Merle and her siblings come to terms with their mother's mental illness and with their own anger and confusion.

Smith, N. (1982). *The Falling Apart Winter*. New York: Walker.

Middle-school adjustment after a family move is compounded for Addam when his mother suffers deepening depression.

Youngest Readers

Chaplan, R. , illust. by M. Chesworth. (1991). *Tell Me a Story, Paint Me the Sun.* New York: Magination Press.

When her father withdraws from her in depression, Sara finds warmth from others, including a teacher and uncle who make her feel special.

Craft, S., and R. Massey, illust. by L. Collins. (1995). *Puzzles, Pictures, and Paper Airplanes: What We Do When Our Parents Get Sick.* South Carolina DMH, 2414 Bull St., Box 485, Columbia, SC 29202. 803-734-7766.

In a school counseling group, Lynda begins to share feelings with others who have a parent with mental illness.

DenBoer, H., illust. by J. Goldstein. (1994). *Please Don't Cry, Mom.* Minneapolis: Carolrhoda Books.

Because his mother is sad all the time, Stephen and his father learn about depression and how to cope with her illness.

Fran, R. (1994). *What's Happened to Mommy?* New York: R. D. Eastman.

Written by a teacher and mother to explain her depressive illness to her children. Centers on a brother and sister and their concerns.

Hamilton, D., illust. by G. Owens. (1995). *Sad Days, Glad Days.* Morton Grove, IL: Albert Whitman.

For children experiencing the confusion of having a parent with severe depression. Offers reassurance that they are not responsible for their parent's illness or its treatment and that their mother loves them in spite of the illness.

Kroll, V., illust. by M. Worcester. (1992). *My Sister, Then and Now.* Minneapolis: Carolrhoda Books.

Ten-year-old Rachel describes how her twenty-year-old sister's schizophrenia has affected the family and expresses her own feelings of sadness and anger.

Liddicut, J., illust. by L. McKay. (1989). *Is Daddy Crazy? An Explanation of Schizophrenia for Children*. Schizophrenia Australia Foundation, 211 Chapel St., Prahran, 3181, Victoria, Australia.

   Simon and Mary are frightened, angry, and confused about their father's strange behavior. The sadness, embarrassment, and sense of loss are addressed along with the potential for individual growth during adversity.

Peterkin, A., illust. by F. Middendorf. (1992). *What About Me? When Brothers and Sisters Get Sick*. New York: Magination Press.

   Laura experiences conflicting emotions when her brother becomes seriously ill. An introduction for parents is especially informative.

Videotapes and Films

Adult Children. (1990). Dallas Alliance for the Mentally Ill. Available from By Hand Productions, 117 Jefferson St., NE, Albuquerque, NM 87108. 1-800-766-4519. Two versions: 30 and 90 mins. $15.00 and $20.00 + $3.00 shipping.

   Six offspring share information and recollections, and discuss the legacy of being raised by a mother or father with mental illness. An insightful and powerful video.

Angela. (1994). Written and directed by Rebecca Miller.

   Angela, age ten, is hurting emotionally in response to the symptoms of her mother's manic depression. Accompanied by her younger sister, she tries to rid herself of sin so that their mother may become better.

Families Coping with Mental Illness. Mental Illness Education Project Videos, 22-D Hollywood Ave., Hohokus, NJ 07423. 1-800-343-5540. Two versions: 22 and 43 mins. Both $54.95. Discounted price for family members: $29.95. Shipping and handling $9.00.

   Participants include ten parents and siblings from Boston. They discuss having a relative with schizophrenia or manic depression and offer suggestions for other family members.

Sanctuary. (1996). Paul Moser, Associate Professor of Theater, Oberlin College, Oberlin, OH 44074. 216-775-8152. 2¾ hrs. $20.00 + $3.00 postage; play manuscript $10.00 (includes postage).

Spans twenty years that cover the progression of Elliot's manic depression, the family's response, and the obstacles—particularly legal—they confront. Narrated by a sibling, with some profanity, the play captures the emotional tides.

Surviving and Thriving with a Mentally Ill Relative. C. Amenson. (1991). San Gabriel, CA: San Gabriel Valley AMI. Available from Paul Burk, 1352 Hidden Springs Lane, Glendora, CA 91741. 818-335-1307. Eight 2-hour videotapes. $12.50 purchase per tape; $5.00 rental. Audiotapes also available.

An excellent series by a knowledgeable professional on causes, treatment, and prognosis. Also offers effective coping skills for family members.

Twist and Shout. (1986). Denmark.

An excellent film that is set with a 1960s soundtrack and centers on the coming of age of two boys. One has a mother with schizophrenia and the other has adolescent conflicts involving romance.

Understanding and Communicating with a Person Who Is Hallucinating, and other educational videotapes. M. Moller. (1989). NurSeminars, Inc., 12204 W. Sunridge Drive, Nine Mile Falls, WA 99026. 509-468-9848. 63 mins. $99.00 purchase; $50.00 rental.

An excellent series of videotapes concerned with serious mental illness. Additional videotapes cover relapse, mania, and delusions.

What's Eating Gilbert Grape? (1993). Starring Johnny Depp.

Gilbert is losing contact with his emotional needs and wants due to his family problems. Over time he assumes responsibility for a brother with a mental disability and a mother with depression.

VIDEOTAPES FOR YOUNG VIEWERS

After the Tears: Teens Talk About Mental Illness in Their Families. (1986). United Mental Health, Inc., 1945 Fifth Avenue, Pittsburgh, PA 15219. 412- 391-3820. 21 mins. $50.00.

Adolescent siblings and offspring share their experiences and suggestions for other teenagers. Also includes interviews with professionals.

Claire's Story. (1994). Wellness Reproductions, Inc., 23945 Mercantile Rd., Suite KX, Beachwood, OH 44122. 1-800-669-9208. Part I, 20 mins; Parts II and III, 28 mins. $199.00.

A unique perspective and indispensable teaching tool concerned with childhood depression for teachers, parents, counselors, and especially children themselves. Includes a handbook for teachers and counselors.

A Different Kind of Illness. (1986). 13 mins. *What About Me.* (1987). 17 mins. New Dimensions Films, 85803 Lorane Highway, Eugene, OR 97405. 1-800-288-4456. $235.00 each.

Designed to help children (ages six to ten) cope with the psychiatric hospitalization of a parent or sibling. Both videotapes use puppets to model the issues and concerns of children.

Kid TV. (1992). Department of Mental Health and Mental Retardation, Division of Training and Certification, Station 80, Box 24, Augusta, ME 04333. 207-287-5876. 17 mins. $25.00.

An innovative video for middle-school students. Includes comedy, rap music, and young journalists in an upbeat program designed to demystify the subject of mental illness.

My Mom Still Loves Me. 20 mins. Package also includes book, *Good Weather or Not,* by Fred Rogers; and Resource Manual. Turtle Creek Valley Mental Health and Mental Retardation Program, Inc., 120 E. 9th Ave., Homestead, PA 15120. 1-800-464-1525. $290.00 package; $15.00 video preview.

Primarily for professionals who are working with children (ages six to ten) who have a parent with mental illness. Package includes a variety of materials and suggestions to assist staff in meeting the needs of young offspring.

ORGANIZATIONS

In addition to the National Alliance for the Mentally Ill, other organizations may be helpful, including the following:

National Depressive and Manic Depressive Association
Box 3395
Chicago, IL 60654
312-939-2442

National Mental Health Association
1021 Prince St.
Alexandria, VA 23314-2971
703-684-7722

Appendix B

NOTES FOR PARENTS
AND FOR PROFESSIONALS

ॐ

Notes for Parents

1. The first order of business is to take care of yourself. Remember the airline instructions about putting on your own oxygen mask before offering assistance to your child. A strong and informed parent is the best insurance that the needs of young family members will be met. Become knowledgeable about mental illness and community resources, learn how to cope with the illness and the mental health system, and develop new sources of support. You will sometimes feel overwhelmed—don't hesitate to reach out to other parents and to professionals. There is much help available.

2. Become familiar with books and articles written about the experiences and needs of young family members. Encourage your child to read books written for his or her age level. Discuss these books and offer an opportunity to ask questions and explore feelings. Arrange for your child to see one of the videotapes designed for children or teenagers.

3. Reach out to your child as early as possible. All young family members are profoundly affected by the mental illness of a beloved parent or sibling. There is no way to shield children from this family event. Even very

young children are sensitive to the stress and disruption in the family. If their needs are ignored, they may develop false and harmful beliefs about the mental illness and their own role in causing it. These risks for young children can be reduced by talking openly about the illness. When asked how they're doing, children often say they are "fine"—but no one is fine under these circumstances. Consider having regular family meetings to discuss the illness and answer questions. Or you may wish to schedule regular sessions with a school psychologist or mental health professional.

4. Encourage your child to ask questions and to share his or her feelings with you. Children need an opportunity to explore feelings of sadness, anger, guilt, and responsibility, and to discuss concerns about their own mental health. They also need reassurance that they are not responsible for the illness. Help them find appropriate ways to contribute to the family. At the same time, reinforce their own growth and development, encourage their interests and activities, and support their plans, hopes, and dreams. Do not let their lives become captive to the mental illness in the family.

5. Meet your child's need for information, skills, and support in an age-appropriate manner. Consult with a mental health professional or school psychologist to get suggestions about what information may be most helpful at a given age and how it should be presented. You may wish to ask a professional to meet with your child on a regular basis to offer information about mental illness and its treatment and to provide suggestions for coping with problems as they arise. Teenagers often worry about the impact of their relative's illness on their own future and may welcome an opportunity to talk about long-term plans. They need reassurance that they can fulfill their family commitments without sacrificing their own lives.

6. Help your child learn to cope with the illness and with his or her feelings about it. Young family members often feel overwhelmed by the powerful emotions surrounding the mental illness, by the unpredictable and frightening symptoms they encounter, and by their own confusion and misinformation. Once they have better understanding of the illness and a sense of how to respond to specific problems and situations, young family members will feel less confused and helpless.

7. Set aside special time for well children so they do not feel neglected or resentful. Perhaps there is someone inside or outside the family who can offer individual attention to your child, such as a grandparent or family friend. Children need to be supported in their schoolwork, in their peer relationships, and in activities outside the family. They often need reassurance that their needs matter. The more people who can offer support and encouragement to young family members, the more likely they are to chart a healthy developmental course.

8. Form a network of parents and mental health professionals committed to meeting the needs of young family members. Contact your local NAMI chapter to locate other parents who share your concern for children and adolescents who are growing up with mental illness in their families. Parents who are coping with similar problems can offer valuable suggestions for meeting your child's needs. Local professionals who work with children and adolescents can offer consultation and services to your parent group.

9. Maintain a life-span perspective that acknowledges your child's changing needs at different stages of development. Seek out services or develop services if none are available. Children and teenagers can benefit from a wide range of services, including educational programs and support groups, as well as personal counseling. At each stage of development, young family members are likely to have new questions and concerns.

10. If no services are available, consider developing services yourself with the assistance of other parents and professionals. For example, young family members can benefit from a specialized group or program that provides information about mental illness, practical advice for coping with everyday problems, and insight into their own experiences. One of the greatest benefits is the opportunity for contact and sharing with other family members. Groups can be offered for elementary, junior high, or high school students, and can be located in a variety of settings, such as a local NAMI office, a school, or a mental health clinic.

11. Consider personal counseling for young family members who are experiencing special difficulty. For some young family members, the mental illness may threaten to overwhelm their own lives and leave them para-

lyzed by feelings of depression, guilt, and hopelessness. These family members may benefit from personal counseling with a school psychologist or a child and adolescent therapist. A consultant at a local mental health center can help you decide whether personal counseling is appropriate for a particular child or teenager.

12. Encourage programs in schools that can educate students and teachers about serious mental illness. Given the incidence of serious mental illness, there are legions of children and adolescents who are living with mental illness in their families. Programs for schoolchildren can increase understanding and reduce stigma. Such programs can also enlist the assistance of teachers, principals, guidance counselors, and school psychologists, who can serve as a support system for your child and other young family members.

Notes for Professionals

1. Become knowledgeable about serious mental illness and its treatment. Learn about the devastating impact of mental illness on families. Identify community resources, including family support and advocacy groups. Armed with this knowledge, you can become an invaluable resource for family members.

2. Be sensitive to the unique perspectives associated with particular family subsystems. Each family member has special experiences, needs, and concerns, including parents, spouses, siblings, children, and even grandparents, aunts, and uncles.

3. Young family members share a special vulnerability to this catastrophic family event, which consumes energy needed for their own growth and development. They have fewer coping resources and strategies than adults and are dependent on other people for meeting their needs. You can work with parents in ensuring that the needs of young family members are met and that their interests, activities, and plans are reinforced.

4. Offer understanding, respect, practical advice, and empathy to these families. Family members continue to report that they receive little attention from professionals and that their own needs are often ignored. A single informed and caring professional can have a positive impact on their lives, especially at the time of the initial diagnosis. You can make a difference!

5. Acknowledge the strengths, resources, and expertise of the families you work with. In the past, based on unsupported theories that blamed families for causing the mental illness, professionals sometimes held families accountable for this family tragedy and added significantly to their burden. Under difficult circumstances, most families are struggling to do their best. You can support their efforts, strengthen their family, and assist them in coping more effectively.

6. Work with parents in meeting the needs of young family members. Especially at the time of the diagnosis, adult members of the family may be so consumed with the demands of the illness that they have little sense of the anguish below the surface in their well children and negligible time or energy for meeting their needs.

7. Ask about the children or teenagers at home and offer to meet with them. In most treatment settings, professional attention is directed toward the person with mental illness and to adult family members who serve as primary caregivers. Little attention is directed toward the young family members at home. Provide regular opportunities for them to ask questions and to share their feelings with you. Reassure them that they are not responsible for the illness.

8. Offer services for children and teenagers in professional settings. They may benefit from an educational program designed to offer information and practical advice or from a support group that allows them to share their feelings and suggestions with other family members. Young family members often worry that their own problems will add to the already overwhelming challenges facing their family, which can add to their feelings of guilt and responsibility. Under these circumstance, a forum outside the family circle can be an invaluable resource.

9. When adult siblings or offspring are involved in their relative's life as primary caregivers or informal case managers, enable them to play an active and informed role in decisions that affect them. Establish a regular channel of communication for family members so that they can remain well informed, ask questions, and offer their observations and insights. Invite them to join the treatment team.

10. Even when adult siblings and offspring do not reside close to their relative, they generally remain concerned and interested. Arrange to have regular contact with these family members by telephone or in person if they are visiting the area. Even at a distance, they can serve as an important source of support for their relative. In addition, they may become more involved in their relative's caregiving in the future as family circumstances change.

11. Visit a family support group and learn about their experiences and needs. In your treatment setting, offer referrals to family organizations in the community, such as NAMI. Offer consultation to family groups in the community, who will welcome programs on mental illness and other professional matters. In turn, you will learn from their experiences and suggestions. If you want to learn about the gaps in the local mental health system, ask family members!

12. Encourage programs about mental illness in schools and work with school personnel in addressing the needs of children and adolescents who are living with mental illness at home. You may wish to work with school psychologists or guidance counselors in offering educational programs or support groups in the school setting. These services can be designed for elementary, junior high, or high school students.

Appendix C

ORGANIZING A
SUPPORT GROUP

꙰

I F YOU WISH to offer services for other siblings and offspring yourself,
initially you should contact your local or state NAMI affiliate to determine the presence of existing services, such as the Journey of Hope
Support and Education Program. If there is no group in your area, you
may want to initiate one. Although it now out of print, A *Group Facilitator's Guide* was developed by Rex. In this section, we share material from
the guide and provide a brief overview of the most important considerations. If you are planning to organize a support group for adult siblings
and offspring, you need to deal with several issues, including publicity,
group format, meeting place, frequency of meetings, group size, and
group membership.

PUBLICITY

There are many ways to publicize your group, including:

- networking among members of your local NAMI or Mental
  Health Association chapter;

- placing public service announcements in your local and alternative papers;

- contacting a sympathetic newspaper reporter to share a personal account or your plans to start a support group;

- developing and distributing fliers at hospitals, libraries, post offices, community centers, mental health centers, academic institutions, laundromats, and supermarkets;

- contacting the clergy and mental health professionals in your community; and

- simply telling people about your group in the course of normal day-to-day conversations—there are lots of siblings and offspring out there.

Group Format

The best group format is one that reflects the size, history, and personality of your group. Through time, your group may choose to modify the format to reflect changing interests and membership. Some of the common formats of various groups are:

- "Telling Our Stories" Group, which allows people to share their personal experiences;

- "Speakers" Group, which includes presentations by invited speakers;

- "Issues" Group, which focuses on issues of particular concern to siblings and offspring;

- "Stage/Step" Group, which is similar to 12-step programs and may use the 8-stage method outlined in Julie Johnson's book, *Hidden Victims;*

- "Professionally Directed" Group, which is initiated or facilitated by a mental health professional; and

- "Journey of Hope" Group, which is led by two trained facilitators (training is offered through your state NAMI affiliate).

Where to Meet

Meeting at a regular time and place will both reduce your work and make it easy for people to remember when and where to come to meetings. Possible sites include:

- a member's home (or alternating houses);

- your local NAMI office, Mental Health Association office, or community mental health center;

- churches or synagogues; and

- schools, libraries, community centers, or apartment clubhouses.

How Often to Meet

Most groups meet once or twice a month, during the week or on Sunday afternoons. Frequency of meetings may vary through time, as interest, enthusiasm, and members change.

Group Size

Many groups begin with a few members and gradually expand. Each size has its advantages. A group of three to six may be intimate; a group of eight to twelve may offer a variety of experiences. Members may also pursue their advocacy efforts through the larger local NAMI group. You can increase group size through publicity and divide a group that seems too large.

Group Membership

Most groups have a core group that attends on a fairly regular basis. They can share tasks and set the agenda for the group. Other members may attend more irregularly or perhaps only briefly, based on their individual needs and desires.

SPECIAL MEMBERS/GUESTS

The focus of your group is the issues and concerns of adult siblings and offspring of people with mental illness. Provided the focus is not diluted, your group may also allow other family members to participate (for example, spouses, nieces, and nephews), as well as spouses or partners of group members. People with mental illness need to be referred to a group that is appropriate for them. Groups for consumers are increasingly available through NAMI, as well as local, state, and national consumer organizations.

FACILITATING MEETINGS

A group facilitator needs to create an atmosphere where people feel safe, know what to expect and have an opportunity to speak about their concerns. Good facilitators generally have the following qualities:

- empathy and caring;

- active listening;

- assertiveness;

- honesty;

- openness;

- a nonjudgmental attitude;

- enjoyment and enthusiasm;

- humor;

- sensitivity;

- energy;

- courage; and

- responsibility.

POTENTIAL ACTIVITIES FOR A FACILITATOR

Facilitators have many roles and responsibilities in the group. Some of the most important include the following:

- delegating responsibilities;

- opening the meeting on time;

- creating a relaxed, interesting, and accepting atmosphere;

- initiating, guiding, and redirecting the discussion;

- keeping the meeting from becoming a therapy session;

- encouraging individuals to talk about themselves, not just the illness;

- holding the group together;

- providing support during crisis situations;

- synthesizing the discussion; and

- closing the meeting on time.

Facilitating meetings is often fun and can help you grow, but you need to remember you are also a member of the group who has personal needs. Your group may want to use a cofacilitator or to rotate the facilitator's responsibilities among members to ensure that everyone's needs are met.

GROUP PROCESS SKILLS

There are a number of essential group process skills, which fall into the following areas:

- feelings, as group members express and share their emotional burden;

- acceptance, as group members create a safe and supportive refuge;

- information, as group members share their accumulated knowledge of relevant books and articles, new research findings, local resources, and coping strategies; and

- reinforcement, as group members give and receive support.

EXPERIMENTATION

Don't be afraid to experiment with the group process. Some possibilities include:

- asking group members to draw their family trees (genograms);

- having members give brief presentations on particular topics;

- watching a relevant film or videotape at a member's home;

- allowing time for a social period before or after the meeting; and

- having special summer or holiday meetings.

RESOURCE MATERIAL

In addition to this book and *Anguished Voices,* a wide range of resources are listed in Appendix A.

SUGGESTED MEETING OUTLINE

There are many ways to structure a support group. For example, the progression of a typical meeting might be as follows:

- introduce yourself and your cofacilitator after asking participants to group themselves in a circle;

- review the group guidelines and other pertinent material;

- ask all members to introduce themselves and state their relationship to their relative with mental illness;

- move into the main part of the meeting (see group format);

- ask if anyone needs special support from the group;

- make announcements about the next meeting and other matters; and

- close the meeting, allowing members to express what was worthwhile for them.

Working Within NAMI

If your group is affiliated with your local NAMI affiliate, you will benefit from membership in a large and effective advocacy organization. You will also become part of a national network of adult siblings and offspring, with the benefits of linking with others.

REFERENCE NOTES

✑

Some of the following references are listed in Appendix A. We have given the full citation for other references the first time they are mentioned. For readers interested in the research literature, many of the books listed in Appendix A have extensive reference lists.

INTRODUCTION

P. xx: our national surveys. Two articles were originally published in *Innovations & Research* (no longer published) and later reprinted elsewhere. See D. Marsh et al., "Anguished voices: Impact of mental illness on siblings and children," reprinted in L. Spaniol (Ed.), 1994, *An Introduction to Rehabilitation Psychology* (pp. 162–175), Columbia, MD: International Association of Psychosocial Rehabilitation Services; and D. Marsh et al., "Troubled journey: Siblings and children of people with mental illness," reprinted in L. Spaniol et al. (Eds.), 1996, *Psychological and Social Aspects of Psychiatric Disability* (pp. 254–269), Boston: Boston University Center for Psychiatric Rehabilitation.

P. xxi: *Anguished Voices*. A book of personal accounts we edited at the same time we were writing *How to Cope with Mental Illness in Your Family*. The eight family members (including Rex) contributed to both books. With their permission, we have selected and edited some brief excerpts for use in this book.

P. xxi: our other research projects. These include D. Marsh et al., 1996, "A person-driven system: Implications for theory, research, and practice," in L. Spaniol et al. (Eds.), *Psychological and Social Aspects of Psychiatric Disability* (pp. 358–369); and D. Marsh et al., 1996, "The family experience of mental illness: Evidence for resilience," *Psychiatric Rehabilitation Journal, 20*(2), 3–12.

P. xxiii: more than five million people. Based on 1996 prevalence data from the Center for Mental Health Services, approximately 5.4 million or 2.7 percent of the adult population have a "severe and persistent" mental illness. For a summary of data concerning the incidence of serious mental illness, see E. F. Torrey, *Surviving Schizophrenia.*

P. xxv: impairments in brain structure and chemistry. For example, see N. Andreasen (Ed.), *Schizophrenia: From Mind to Molecule*; E. F. Torrey, *Surviving Schizophrenia*; and E. F. Torrey et al., *Schizophrenia and Manic-Depressive Illness.*

Pp. xxvi–xxviii: schizophrenia, major depression, and manic depression. Material regarding these mental illnesses was adapted from the most current and widely used diagnostic system, the fourth edition of the *Diagnostic and Statistical Manual of Mental Disorders* (DSM-IV), 1994, Washington, DC: American Psychiatric Association.

P. xxviii: 50 percent of people. D. Regier et al., 1990, "Comorbidity of mental disorders with alcohol and other drug abuse: Results from the Epidemiologic Catchment Area (ECA) Study," *Journal of the American Medical Association, 264,* 2511–2528. See helpful discussions of substance abuse in K. Mueser and S. Gingerich, *Coping with Schizophrenia;* and H. Ryglewicz and B. Pepper, 1996, *Lives at Risk: Understanding and Treating Young People with Dual Disorders,* New York: Free Press.

P. xxx: three essential elements of hope. C. Snyder, 1994, *The Psychology of Hope: You Can Get There From Here,* New York: Free Press.

CHAPTER 1: YOUR JOURNEY OF HOPE AND HEALING

P. 1: naming and taming. C. Monahon, 1993, *Children and Trauma: A Parent's Guide to Helping Children Heal,* New York: Lexington. An excellent discussion of childhood trauma.

P. 2: Father's Day. L. Parker, 1995, "When the music stopped," *The Washington Post,* June 18, p. C3.

Pp. 9–10: potential risks. For a discussion of psychological trauma and its treatment, see J. Herman, 1992, *Trauma and Recovery,* New York: Basic Books. For a discussion of emotional flooding, see E. Waites, 1993, *Trauma and Survival,* New York: Norton.

Pp. 11–13: strategies for using this book. Many resources can assist you in handling the material in *How to Cope with Mental Illness in Your Family*. For example, see the books and videotapes listed in Appendix A. You can develop your skills by reading self-help books or taking courses in stress management, assertiveness, conflict management, etc. Many self-help materials are available from New Harbinger Publications, Inc., 5674 Shattuck Ave., Oakland, CA 94609. 1-800-748-6273. For trainers, educators, and group leaders, a resource is Whole Person Associates, Inc., 210 West Michigan, Duluth, MN 55802. 1-800-247-6789. In addition, many books are available, such as J. Kabat-Zinn, 1990, *Full Catastrophe Living: Using the Wisdom of Your Body and Mind to Face Stress, Pain, and Illness*, New York: Delta.

CHAPTER 2: REVISITING YOUR CHILDHOOD

P. 20: how mental illness disrupts the family. For information concerned with the family experience of mental illness, see Appendix A.

P. 24: chronic sorrow. Originally proposed to explain the parental response to a child's disability by S. Olshansky, 1962, "Chronic sorrow: A response to having a mentally defective child," *Social Casework, 43,* 190–193. Discussed in D. Marsh, *Families and Mental Illness.*

P. 26: violent or self-destructive behavior. See E. F. Torrey, *Surviving Schizophrenia*. Statistics on television portrayals from W. Dubin & P. Fink, 1992, "Effects of stigma on psychiatric treatment," in P. Fink and A. Tasman (Eds.), *Stigma and Mental Illness* (pp. 1–7), Washington, DC: American Psychiatric Press. Suicide rates from DSM-IV.

P. 26: death rate from suicide and other causes of death. M. Berren et al., 1994, "Serious mental illness and mortality rates," *Hospital and Community Psychiatry, 45,* 604–605.

P. 27: pay the price. M. Rosenson et al., 1988, "Expanding the role of families of the mentally ill," in J. McNeil & S. Weinstein (Eds.), *Innovations: In Health Care Practice* (pp. 116–133), Silver Spring, MD: National Association of Social Workers.

Pp. 27–29: services. See E. F. Torrey, *Surviving Schizophrenia* for documentation of these statistics and a general discussion of services.

P. 29: stigma. Discussion based in part on a still relevant report on stigma and mental illness. Task Panel Report, 1978, "Access and barriers to care, in *The Presidents Commission on Mental Heath* (Vol. 2), Washington, DC: U. S. Government Printing Office. Also see P. Fink & A. Tasman (Eds.), *Stigma and Mental Illness.*

P. 29: mass media. See O. Wahl, 1995, *Media Madness: Public Images of Mental Illness,* New Brunswick, NJ: Rutgers University Press.

P. 33: maladaptive coping strategies. See C. Figley, 1989, *Helping Traumatized Families,* San Francisco: Jossey-Bass.

P. 34–36: family resilience. For discussion of family strengths, see C. Dunst et al. (Eds.), 1994, *Supporting and Strengthening Families. Vol. 1: Methods, Strategies and Practices,* Cambridge, MA: Brookline. Also see D. Marsh, *Families and Mental Illness.* Some of the experiential material in this section taken from D. Marsh et al., 1996, "The family experience of mental illness: Evidence for resilience," *Psychiatric Rehabilitation Journal, 20* (2), 3–12.

Pp. 37–43: individual family members. See material in Appendix A, especially M. Wasow, *The Skipping Stone.*

Pp. 37–38: your relative with mental illness. See A. Hatfield & H. Lefley, *Surviving Mental Illness,* as well as the first-person accounts that appear regularly in *Schizophrenia Bulletin.* Experiential material in this section taken from D. Marsh et al., 1996, "A person-driven system: Implications for theory, research, and practice," in L. Spaniol et al. (Eds.), *Psychological and Social Aspects of Psychiatric Disability* (pp. 358–369).

Pp. 38–40: parents. See material in Appendix A. Also see D. Marsh, *Families and Mental Illness* (quote on pp. 39–40 from p. 10); and M. Wasow, *The Skipping Stone.*

P. 40: spouses. See D. Marsh, *Families and Mental Illness* (quote on p. 40 from p. 133); and M. Wasow, *The Skipping Stone.* Some vignettes taken from E. Mannion, 1996, "Resilience and burden in spouses of people with mental illness," *Psychiatric Rehabilitation Journal, 20* (2), 13–23.

Pp. 41–42: siblings; offspring; multigenerational family members. See material in Appendix A.

P. 43: other relatives. See M. Wasow, *The Skipping Stone.*

CHAPTER 3: RECLAIMING YOUR CHILDHOOD

P. 47: vulnerability of young family members. For a developmental model concerned with the impact of illness and disability on families, see J. Rolland, 1994, *Families, Illness, and Disability,* New York: Basic Books.

P. 54: parentification. See E. Brown, *My Parent's Keeper.*

P. 55: replacement child syndrome. The replacement child syndrome was originally proposed in connection with sibling bereavement in E. Poznanski, 1972, "The 'replacement child': A saga of unresolved parental grief," *Journal of Pediatrics, 81,* 1190–1193.

P. 55: survivor's syndrome. For example, see R. Lifton, 1993, *The Protean Self: Human Resilience in an Age of Fragmentation,* New York: Basic Books.

P. 60: straddling two worlds. For a discussion of this issue among siblings of children with disabilities, see H. Featherstone, 1980, *A Difference in the Family: Living with a Disabled Child,* New York: Penguin; T. Powell & P. Gallagher, 1993, *Brothers and Sisters: A Special Part of Exceptional Families* (2nd ed.), Baltimore: Brookes; and M. Seligman & R. Darling, 1989, *Ordinary Families, Special Children: A Systems Approach to Childhood Disability,* New York: Guilford.

P. 63: increased risk of developing mental illness yourself. Genetic risks are discussed in I. Gottesman, 1991, *Schizophrenia Genesis: The Origins of Madness.* For example, the risk of developing schizophrenia is 13% for an offspring, 9% for a sibling, 5% for a grandchild, and 4% for a niece or nephew. Genetic risks are also discussed in E. F. Torrey, *Surviving Schizophrenia.*

Pp. 63–65: personal resilience. See G. Higgins, 1994, *Resilient Adults: Overcoming a Cruel Past,* San Francisco: Jossey-Bass; and S. Wolin & S. Wolin, 1993, *The Resilient Self: How Survivors of Troubled Families Rise Above Adversity,* New York: Villard. Some of our discussion is based on material in these books.

CHAPTER 4: REFLECTING ON YOUR CURRENT LIFE

P. 68: developmental tasks of adulthood. Again, for a useful developmental model, see J. Rolland, *Families, Illness, and Disability.*

P. 72: twinship. For research concerned with the landmark study of identical twins, see E. F. Torrey et al., *Schizophrenia and Manic-Depressive Disorder.*

P. 73: looking-glass self. C. Cooley's concept is discussed in R. Janoff-Bulman, 1992, *Shattered Assumptions,* New York: Free Press.

P. 74: psychic numbing. For further discussion of psychic numbing, see books on psychological trauma, including J. Herman, *Trauma and Recovery*; A. Matsakis, 1992, *I Can't Get Over It: A Handbook for Trauma Survivors*, Oakland, CA: New Harbinger; C. Monahon, 1993, *Children and Trauma: A Parent's Guide to Helping Children Heal;* and E. Waites, *Trauma and Survival: Post-Traumatic and Dissociative Disorders in Women.*

P. 80: early researchers. J. Clausen and M. Yarrow (Eds.), 1955, "The impact of mental illness on the family [special issue]," *Journal of Social Issues, 11*(4).

P. 84: shadows your parenthood. For information regarding genetic risks, see I. Gottesman, *Schizophrenia Genesis: The Origins of Madness*; and E. F. Torrey, *Surviving Schizophrenia.*

P. 85: caregiving. See H. Lefley, *Family Caregiving in Mental Illness,* for a comprehensive discussion of this topic.

CHAPTER 5: RESOLVING YOUR LEGACY

P. 91: phases of adaptation. Adapted from T. Rando, 1984, *Grief, Dying, and Death: Clinical Interventions for Caregivers,* Champaign, IL: Research Press.

Pp. 94–96: traumatic and posttraumatic reactions. See books on trauma noted above. A useful self-help book is A. Matsakis, 1992, *I Can't Get Over It: A Handbook for Trauma Survivors.*

P. 96: factors affecting your adaptation process. Many excellent books concerned with family coping and adaptation are available. See Appendix A.

P. 104: joining a support group. Contact NAMI about the availability of a support group in your area. Also see J. Johnson, *Hidden Victims.*

P. 107: potential benefits and risks. There is a large body of literature documenting the effectiveness of psychotherapy. For example, see results of a psychotherapy survey of 7000 subscribers reported in *Consumer Reports* ("Mental health: Does therapy help?," 1995, November, pp. 734–739); and A. Roth and P. Fonagy, 1996, *What Works for Whom?: A Critical Review of Psychotherapy Research,* New York: Guilford. On the negative side, see discussion of risks for family members in D. Marsh, *Families and Mental Illness.*

CHAPTER 6: REVISING THE LEGACY

P. 118: courage. For a discussion of the role of courage in change, see D. Waters & E. Lawrence, 1993, *Competence, Courage, and Change: An Approach to Family Therapy,* New York: Norton.

P. 121: appraisal. For more information on appraisal, see R. Janoff-Bulman, *Shattered Assumptions*; A. Monat & R. Lazarus (Eds.), 1991, *Stress and Coping: An Anthology,* New York: Columbia University Press; and S. Taylor, *Positive Illusions,* 1989, New York: Basic Books.

P. 121: M. Bateson, 1990, *Composing a Life,* New York: Atlantic Monthly.

P. 128: mental health system. For additional information on the mental health system, see E. F. Torrey, *Surviving Schizophrenia.*

P 131: state hospital census. Figures taken from E. F. Torrey, *Surviving Schizophrenia.*

P. 132: our present objective. See R. Hunter & D. Marsh, "Mining giftedness," in D. Marsh (Ed.), 1994, *New Directions in the Psychological Treatment of Serious Mental Illness* (pp. 99–122), Westport, CT: Praeger.

P. 132: family-professional relationships. See H. Lefley, "Family-professional relationships," in D. Marsh (Ed.), *New Directions in the Psychological Treatment of Serious Mental Illness* (pp. 166–185); H. Lefley & M. Wasow, *Helping Families Cope with Mental Illness*; and D. Marsh, *Families and Mental Illness.*

P. 135: institutional alliance with families. H. Grunebaum & H. Friedman, 1988, "Building collaborative relationships with families of the mentally ill," *Hospital and Community Psychiatry, 39,* 1183–1187.

P. 136: confidentiality. See A. Zipple et al., 1990, "Client confidentiality and the family's need to know: Strategies for resolving the conflict," *Community Mental Health Journal, 26,* 533–545.

Pp. 137–140: forging a resilient path. Some of our suggestions are based on material in G. Higgins, *Resilient Adults*; and S. Wolin & S. Wolin, *The Resilient Self.*

CHAPTER 7: RENEWING YOUR LIFE

Pp. 147–149: enrich our lives. See K. Jamison, 1993, *Touched with Fire: Manic-Depressive Illness and the Artistic Temperament,* New York: Free Press.

Pp. 148–149: reconnecting with your relative. For insights into the experience of mental illness, see Appendix A, especially A. Hatfield and H. Lefley, *Surviving Mental Illness*; and K. Jamison, *An Unquiet Life: A Memoir of Moods and Madness.* Also see the personal accounts in *Schizophrenia Bulletin.*

P. 149: some excellent resources. See Appendix A.

P. 158: alcohol and drug abuse. See K. Mueser and S. Gingerich, *Coping with Schizophrenia;* and H. Ryglewicz and B. Pepper, 1996, *Lives at Risk: Understanding and Treating Young People with Dual Disorders.*

P. 160: planning for the future. See K. Mueser and S. Gingerich, *Coping with Schizophrenia;* and E. F. Torrey, *Surviving Schizophrenia.* Also contact NAMI for information about long-term planning.

INDEX

ABOUT THE AUTHOR

❧

DIANE T. MARSH, PH.D., is Professor of Psychology at the University of Pittsburgh at Greensburg. She specializes in professional practice with people who have serious mental illness and with their families. Dr. Marsh is the author of *Families and Mental Illness: New Directions in Professional Practice* (Praeger, 1992) and *Families and Mental Retardation: New Directions in Professional Practice* (Praeger, 1992); the editor of *New Directions in the Psychological Treatment of Serious Mental Illness* (Praeger, 1994); the coeditor of *Ethical and Legal Issues in Professional Practice with Families* (Wiley, 1997); and a coauthor of *The Role of the Family in Psychiatric Disability* (Boston University Center for Psychiatric Rehabilitation, 1997). Active nationally as a psychologist, advocate, and workshop presenter, Dr. Marsh is a member of the American Psychological Association Task Force on Serious Mental Illness. She is also active as a member of the National Alliance for the Mentally Ill (NAMI).

ABOUT THE AUTHOR

REX M. DICKENS has an undergraduate degree in chemical engineering and a master's degree in business administration. He has served as an Air Force pilot and has been employed as an engineer, a commuter pilot, and a commodity floor clerk. This background provided little assistance as he witnessed his mother and three siblings develop serious mental illness. His personal account of this experience is contained in *Anguished Voices* (Boston University Center for Psychiatric Rehabilitation, 1994), which he edited with Dr. Marsh. In 1984 he began one of the first self-help groups for adult siblings and offspring in California. Since that time Mr. Dickens has served on the national board of the former Siblings and Adult Children (SAC) Network of NAMI, developed publications, written articles and reviews, and presented workshops within the NAMI organization. He has recently relocated to Hedrick, Iowa.